LISTEN FOR SUCCESS
A Guide to Effective Listening

Arthur K. Robertson, Ph.D.

Professional Publishing
Burr Ridge, Illinois
New York, New York

This publication is designed to provide accurate and
authoritative information in regard to the subject matter
covered. It is sold with the understanding that neither the
author nor the publisher is engaged in rendering legal, accounting,
or other professional service. If legal advice or other expert
assistance is required, the services of a competent professional
person should be sought.

From a Declaration of Principles jointly adopted by a Committee
of the American Bar Association and a Committee of Publishers.

Sponsoring editor:	Cynthia A. Zigmund
Project editor:	Jane Lightell
Production manager:	Laurie Kersch
Designer:	Larry J. Cope
Art manager:	Kim Meriwether
Compositor:	Wm. C. Brown Communications, Inc.
Typeface:	11/13 Palatino
Printer:	The Book Press

Library of Congress Cataloging-in-Publication Data

Robertson, Arthur K.

   Listen for success: a guide to effective listening / Arthur K.
Robertson.
     p. cm.—(The Briefcase books series)
   Includes bibliographical references.
   ISBN 1–55623–830–4   0-7863-0203-8 (Paperback)
   1. Listening. 2. Interpersonal communication. 3. Success in
business. 4. Success. I. Title. II. Series.
  BF323.L5R63   1994
  153.6'8—dc20   93–14441

Printed in the United States of America

1 2 3 4 5 6 7 8 9 0   BP   0 9 8 7 6 5 4 3

To my son Scott, an excellent listener

The Briefcase Books Series

Managing Stress: Keeping Calm Under Fire
Barbara J. Braham

Business Negotiating Basics
Peter Economy

Straight Answers to People Problems
Fred E. Jandt

Empowering Employees through Delegation
Robert B. Nelson

The Presentation Primer: Getting Your Point Across
Robert B. Nelson
Jennifer Wallick

Listen for Success: A Guide to Effective Listening
Arthur K. Robertson

Preface

Former labor secretary Ray Donovan once told the Financial Analysts Federation of an early experience in investing. "I've learned that you have to listen very carefully to what financial analysts and investment advisors tell you. This comes as a result of 25-years' experience with advisors, many of whom are in this room, I'm sure. But I did have a meeting with my investment advisor one day back; in the good old days before I entered government I had some money to invest, and I asked him if a particular investment was a good idea. He says, 'Ray, you stand to make a lot of money out of that investment.'

"I thanked him. I went back home. I discussed it with my wife and put a fairly large sum of money into the deal. In six weeks I lost every penny of it. So I went back to that advisor, and I started to complain about the advice he gave. He looked me straight in the eye and said, 'Ray, I gave you good advice. The trouble is you just didn't listen. I said you'd make money *out* of that deal, not in it.' "

Ineffective listening costs money!

Effective listening is the number one communication skill requisite to success in your professional and personal life. The benefits include greater productivity, better understanding, increased job potential, and more operating efficiency. Then add the reduction of wasted time and materials.

Yet in our hurry-up society pressure mounts to get more things done in less time, and it has never been more difficult to be an effective listener.

Approximately 70 percent of our Fortune 500 companies have listening training programs, but 70 percent of the managers in those companies are perceived to be only fair listeners. This book was written to guide you through the successful process that has helped thousands of managers and professionals become more effective listeners. Our listening program provides a way that participants can translate what they learn from this book into real life applications at work and at home.

Language is defined in the *Oxford American Dictionary* as a system of signs and symbols used for conveying information. Through what I call The Language of Effective Listening the effective listener conveys to the speaker an understanding of the speaker's message. This self-help book is for people who want to improve their communication with the significant people in their lives. With just 20 minutes reading per day, you will gain sufficient new techniques to immediately apply in your regular communication activities. We equip you to identify skills to practice in the real world. The *payoff* comes with your practice.

Many of the principles in the early chapters will not strike you as new. Rather these chapters bring to conscious awareness principles learned early in your language development. To this newfound awareness, you will add the means to apply your knowledge to your best advantage. Through reflection and practice of the exercises provided, your level of awareness of effective listening skills is raised regarding most of the material presented. This sense of familiarity will raise your level of comfort with the material and make it easier to apply.

To help yourself, you are asked to identify five people with whom you would like to build better communication. Choose some from your professional environment and others from your personal relationships. Think of these five persons consistently as you read the book. Immediately after a reading session, try to practice the skills you are learning when communicating with these individuals. Specific application of what the book teaches increases your potential for success.

Frequently, humorous anecdotes illustrate a principle. Learning is more enjoyable and therefore much easier if you are able to laugh once in a while. The ancient theory that laughter is good medicine actually has a physiological basis. The *American Medical Association Bulletin* reports that every organ of the body responds to laughter. According to *American Health*, it works this way, "the pituitary gland shoots out endorphins, chemical cousins of such painkilling drugs as heroin and morphine. Lachrymal glands of the eyes produce tears. The zygomatic muscles in the head contort as if in pain. The lower jaw vibrates lickety-bang. The arteries relax after tensing. Vocal cords undergo spasms and produce sound. The heart increases its pace, meeting immediate oxygen needs. Lungs build pressure before releasing air. The diaphragm tightens for spasms of respiration. From the nervous system comes a deluge of adrenaline, which ensues in euphoria. Abdominal muscles double like a fist. Leg muscles relax, causing a weakening feeling. " Science is only in the preliminary stages of isolating the tremendous benefits of laughter.

Laughter is a metaphor for the entire range of positive emotions: faith, hope, love, the will to live, cheer, humor, creativity, playfulness, confidence, great expectations. Positive thoughts are the launching pad for making healthy relationships at work and at home. Healthy relationships increase productivity. Happy people laugh up to 400 times a day.

The positive feelings that ensue from a moment of laughter are fleeting. The positive results that come from using the Language of Effective Listening with the most significant people in your life will last. So the jokes and cartoons are an attempt to keep you moving toward the greater benefits. As John the Apostle said, "We are writing that your joy may be complete."

First, there is a compilation of bits and pieces from the lives of a variety of people that we have known. Then comes self-analysis. Measured by a proven criterion, how well do you listen? After identifying problem areas, you are introduced to solutions. Easy to follow techniques assist you to replace bad habits with good ones.

You also see how the benefits of effective listening touch every area of your life. Your personal autonomy, productivity, and relationships are all influenced by more effective listening.

Understanding the speaker's purpose in talking and learning how to respond appropriately to the various purposes saves you time and increases your value to your business, family, friends, and associates. You can reduce stress by becoming aware of where breakdowns in communication in the past, present, or future occur and how to repair them. Previously difficult relationships can become positive ones as you apply the RELATIONS model. Furthermore, you can raise the esteem of those who communicate with you.

Emotions—their power, their effect on communication, and the know-how of their control is discussed in detail. In the hundreds of conversations we have in a typical day, we try to influence someone with our thinking. Another chapter shows that the Language of Effective Listening is a dynamic persuasion tool. Not a tool of manipulation, effective listening enables you to listen with integrity yet persuasively to the important people in your life.

Some researchers suggest that up to 90 percent of the meaning of communication is nonverbal body language. Chapter 9 enables you to identify the meaning of nonverbal communication so that you will read the communication of the five people you have identified with understanding.

Note taking is a skill that effective listeners use to increase retention. Apply the lessons of Chapter 10 on note taking to increase retention and become more responsible in fulfilling obligations.

The conclusion reviews and summarizes the action plan that, if followed, brings you maximum benefit from using this book. On the back page, you find a tear out return card to complete and mail for more information about a training session for your organization.

May God bless you as you pursue the benefits of the Language of Effective Listening!

Acknowledgments

I am grateful to Mary Ann Orman who, in 1978, while on the staff at AT&T, telephoned and invited me to research, develop, and present a workshop to AT&T corporate managers on effective listening. In this way, I underwent the metamorphosis of becoming a more effective listener myself and became well prepared to share the methodology with others, which I have found to be a real enjoyment.

My program would not have been a success without the generous contribution of "The Ambassador of Listening," Dr. Lyman K. Steil. "Manny" was chairman of the Department of Rhetoric at the University of Minnesota and founder of the International Listening Association, and he is now the president of Communication Development, Inc. He gave me the opportunity to learn from his academic research on effective listening. Giving me the benefit of his own practical experience, always embellished with his own outstanding character, he guaranteed that this willing disciple would be successful in learning and teaching this important skill. Thank you Manny!

In addition, I am very thankful to the many thousands of managers and professionals within IBM, AT&T, and the other Fortune 100 companies who responded enthusiastically to my teaching methods and material. I learned as much from listening to them as they did from listening to me.

Thanks also to Dr. Ken Boa for his numerous insights and encouragement as a teaching colleague. Thanks to Roger Petersen for the humorous touch and his drawings of the various facial expressions. A special thanks to the Reverend Jay Sidebotham for his excellent cartoons, sprinkled throughout the text. Thanks to Bill Proctor for faithfully reflecting my thoughts in the opening and closing narratives.

I am indebted to several who gave thoughtful and helpful criticism to the early manuscript. They deserve credit for the clarity and accuracy of the text. Where problems or mistakes still exist, I take full responsibility for not always following their excellent advice. Sincere thanks are extended to Dr. Suzette Haden Elgin, professor of psycholinguistics emeritus, San Diego State College; Dr. Bernard G. Guerney, Jr., professor of human development at Pennsylvania State University and head of Individual and Family Consultation Center; Tom Taylor, professor of biblical languages at Biblical Theological Seminary; Tom Dunkerton, retired senior vice president of Saatchi, Saatchi and Compton; Lourene Clark, vice president executive development of Citicorp; and Joe Moore, manager of human resources at R. R. Donnelley.

Many thanks to Stephany Hull, who took time out from an already full schedule, to work long hours over a short period of weeks to craft my first draft into a respectable manuscript. A special thanks to Gene Kucharsky for his masterful condensing, editing, and chapter titles.

I am grateful to Marilyn Pritchard for putting the manuscript into final form for submission to the publisher.

Bob Nelson told me of the opportunity to write this book and then advised, tactfully admonished, and encouraged me to complete it. His editorial role in the final draft has helped considerably. Thanks also to Ken Blanchard, "The One Minute Manager" who wanted to see me write this book. His encouragement by words and example is appreciated!

Most of all, thanks to my wonderful wife, Linda, a true woman of Prov. 31, "Who is more precious than jewels." Her love, prayers, dedication, and support made it possible for me to leave a secure college teaching position and embark on the successful adventure of learning and teaching these skills in the corporate community. Linda has taught me to listen to the heart as well as to the mind.

Arthur K. Robertson

Briefcase Books — Series Introduction

Research shows that people who buy business books (1) want books that can be read quickly, perhaps on a plane trip, commuting on a train, or overnight, and (2) feel their time and money were well spent if they get two or three useful insights or techniques for improving their professional skills or helping them with a current problem at work.

Briefcase Books were designed to meet these two criteria. They focus on necessary skills and problem areas, and include real-world examples from practicing managers and professionals. Inside these books you'll find useful, practical information and techniques in a straightforward, concise, and easy-to-read format.

This book and others like it in the Briefcase Books series can quickly give you insights and answers regarding your current needs and problems. And they are useful references for future situations and problems.

If you find this book or any other in this series to be of value, please share it with your coworkers. With tens of thousands of new books published each year, any book that can simplify the growing complexities in manaing others needs to be circulated as widely as possible.

Robert B. Nelson
Series Editor

Foreword for the Briefcase Books Series

My mission in life has been to be a conveyor of simple truths. It is for that reason that I'm pleased to be able to introduce the Briefcase Books series, which seeks to provide simple, practical and direct answers to the most common problems managers face on a daily basis.

It has been my experience that in the field of business common sense is not common practice. So it is refreshing to find a series of books that glorifies common sense in dealing with people in the workplace.

Take the skill of listening. We all know that it is important to listen, yet how many of us actually do it well? I suggest it would be rare to find one in a hundred managers that is truly a good listener. Most people focus on what they are going to say next when someone else is talking. They would seldom if ever think to check what they thought they heard to make sure it is accurate. And they seldom acknowledge or attempt to deal with emotions when they occur in speaking with someone at work. These are basic errors in the use of this basic skill. And regardless of how much education or experience you have, you should know how to listen.

But how much training have you had on the topic of listening? Have you ever had a course on the topic? Have you ever tested your ability to listen? Have you ever discussed with others how you could listen better with greater comprehension and respect? Probably not. Even though this fundamental interpersonal skill could cripple the most talented individual if he or she is not good at it.

Fortunately, listening is just one of the fundamental skills singled out for its own volume in the Briefcase Books series. Others include books on making presentations, negotiating, problem solving, and handling stress. And other volumes are planned even as I write this.

The Briefcase Books series focuses on those basic skills that managers must master to excel at work. Whether you are new to managing or are a seasoned manager, you'll find these books of value in obtaining useful insights and fundamental knowledge you can use for your entire career.

Ken Blanchard
Coauthor
The One Minute Manager

Contents

Chapter One

A Tale of Two Managers

It is through experiencing your acceptance, respect and appreciation that the other will become more open and honest with you and thereby increase your ability to be helpful and to resolve possible problems and conflicts with the other.

—Dr. Bernard G. Guerney, Jr., *Relationship Enhancement: Marital/Family Therapist's Manual*

Barb and Bob worked in the same office, and both were considered by many to be on the fast track to the top of ABC Company. They were about the same age, in their mid-30s, and were hard workers. The pair had made equally significant contributions to the profits of their company. They both had reputations as creative thinkers, incisive analysts, and excellent planners. Both had graduated near the top of their college classes. Yet with all their similarities, a major difference emerged in their career paths. Barb eventually was promoted to the ranks of senior management. Bob wasn't.

Why did Barb stay on the fast track while Bob got derailed? In a word, Barb learned to build strong supportive relationships on the job through what I call the *Language of Effective Listening*. Bob, in contrast, failed to master this language, and his career suffered as a result. See how quickly you can pick up the pivotal clues in the following episodes.

BOB'S TALE

When Bob arrived at his office one morning, he was told by his secretary that his boss, Sam, wanted to see him. But Bob was preoccupied by a near-accident during his commute to work. He brushed off his secretary and went immediately into his office. Just as he closed his door she managed to call out, "Sam did say he wanted to talk with you as soon as possible!"

Bob didn't pick up this final part of the message. He assumed there wasn't any particular urgency to the matter. So he spent a few minutes tidying up his desk, taking care of several other things, and replaying in his mind the sequence of events that led up to the accident.

When Bob finally walked into Sam's office about 45 minutes later, he got the picture that his boss's message was urgent.

"Where have you been?" shouted Sam, a volatile and impatient type. "You're always late! Look, I've got to have that Smith report you've been working on—*now*!"

"I was in the office," Bob said. He folded his arms across his chest, crossed his legs, and shifted his body slightly to the side. He didn't like to be on the receiving end of this sort of criticism. He had the uncomfortable sense that Sam had pushed him into a kind of fortress and was now battering away verbally, trying to wound him.

"If you were in your office, why didn't you come over here to see me?" Sam pressed. "Didn't you get my message?"

"Sure I got it, but . . ."

"But you didn't think it was that important? Look, Bob, your performance on this project could go a long way toward making your future in this company. You've been doing a pretty good job so far, so don't blow it. Now, be sure you get me that report before noon, okay?"

Bob left this meeting angry, upset, and a little frightened. And the first person he released his emotions on was his secretary, "Why didn't you tell me Sam's message was so urgent?" he said through clenched teeth.

"I tried to," she responded. "But you were in such a hurry you closed your door before I could explain."

"Well stop me next time and get the full message across. That's your job! Understand?"

His secretary nodded glumly, but this sort of confrontation had occurred with Bob too often in the past for her to accept his criticism easily. In fact, this accusation pushed her over the edge. Within days she turned in her resignation.

As for Sam, this recent encounter with Bob just confirmed a feeling that he had been developing. Bob didn't seem to operate gracefully under the pressures that burden those in responsible management positions.

BARB'S TALE

The same morning, Barb arrived at ABC Company at almost exactly the same time Bob did. In fact, they rode up the elevator together. Barb was feeling some pressure that day, too. When she dropped off her son at his kindergarten class, he had been feeling sick, and she was worried about him. The problem could be his usual car sickness, she thought, but then again, maybe he's coming down with the flu that was going around.

As she passed her secretary, she was mulling over a decision to call the school nurse and ask her to keep an eye on the boy. But her secretary interrupted her thought, "Sam wants to see you about the Jones project."

Barb acknowledged the message and kept walking toward her office. But then she stopped and consciously "shifted gears" mentally. She realized she didn't have enough information to respond appropriately to this message, so she asked the secretary, "Did he say when he wants to see me?"

"First thing this morning."

"Okay, buzz his office and tell him I'll be right in," Barb said.

She immediately went into her own office, called the school nurse, and took care of the problem with her son. She hadn't felt she could delegate this important family concern. Besides, she knew it would only take a minute or two to notify the nurse. Also, by instructing her secretary to call Sam and let him know she was coming, she was able to keep the boss calm.

When Barb walked into Sam's office about five minutes later, the first thing he said was, "I've got your report on the Jones project, and it's not adequate. We can't lose this client, Barb, and I've been counting on you to come through for us. Success with this project could be a feather in your cap for your future here at ABC. But if you blow this, it could really look bad. Tell me, did you really put in some quality time on this?"

"Sam, I know this project is very important," Barb replied calmly. "I've put it at the top of my list of things to do. But remember, you've also given me three other projects that are 'top priority.' I'm convinced that I can do a good job on all of them, but I sense that at this point, I need your expertise and guidance to back me up."

"What can I do?" Sam asked, leaning toward her.

"First of all, let's agree on how we're going to juggle all these projects so that they all get finished successfully and on time," Barb replied, leaning slightly toward him. "Then, I'd like to go over exactly what changes you want on the Jones project report." At that, Barb pulled out a note pad so that she could jot down Sam's instructions and suggestions.

When Barb returned to her office, she decided she should also pass on a little constructive criticism to her secretary.

"Let me share something with you that you should know, because you're an important member of this team," Barb began confidentially. "Sam is a little nervous about some of the projects we're working on, and rightly so, because they're important to the profit picture of the company. He has put a lot of trust in you and me, and that's why we're working with some of the most significant clients this company has.

"So be sure when you give me a message from him, or from anyone else, for that matter, that I get all of it at once. Okay? In fact, I think it will be best to write down the main points and hand the note to me as soon as you see me. You'll recall I had to ask you this morning *when* Sam wanted to see me. I would like that information without having to ask for it.

"I do know you have a lot to think about, though, and believe me, I wouldn't give these responsibilities to anyone else. I've made it clear to Sam and the other management people how valuable you are, and that's one of the reasons you're so well paid. I personally appreciate how well you're supporting me under all this pressure."

Barb's secretary *didn't* quit her job; in fact, she stayed with Barb throughout her later rise in the ABC Company hierarchy. Also, Sam felt quite good about the meeting with Barb, especially her willingness to do her job cheerfully and diligently, even when she was operating under a lot of pressure. And he was gratified at her apparent respect for him and his abilities.

A Lesson in the Language of Effective Listening

These two scenarios could be interpreted several different ways. Some might argue that Barb's primary strength was that she was better prepared emotionally to deal with the stresses of life than was Bob. Others might say that she was a better-organized person. Still others might contend that she was more mature, more confident, or simply a nicer person.

All this may be true, but there is something even more significant. The master key to Barb's handling of those challenging situations that morning and to her upward movement

in her organization was that she had learned to use effectively and powerfully the Language of Effective Listening.
Bob, in contrast, seemed to know almost nothing about this
special language.

Specifically, Barb showed that she had learned these lessons about the Language of Effective Listening:

• She did not allow outside "noises," preoccupations, or
daydreams to intrude on her ability to listen. She was rightly
concerned about her son's nausea at school. But she was able
to give a priority to that problem and still focus on the
message her secretary was communicating from her boss,
Sam.

• She knew how to accept criticism from Sam by "filter-
ing" the truth, the emotional factors, and the attempts at
threatening, bullying, or persuading in his statements. In
this way, she was able to gain a sense of perspective on his
criticism, evaluate it, and respond constructively.

• Barb was able to establish quick rapport with Sam,
despite his initial hostility. Using the proper words as well
as the body signals of the Language of Effective Listening,
she gave him the impression that it would be worthwhile
and pleasant for him to build a working relationship with
her.

• She also passed on constructive criticism to her secretary
about how to convey messages. Far from feeling threatened, the
secretary went away from the discussion with a sense that Barb
valued her work and professional ability.

In achieving this result, Barb had observed, among other
things, the "five-to-one" rule. That is, she mentioned five
positive points about the secretary (count them!) to the one
criticism she offered. By weighting her negative observation
so heavily with affirmations, Barb ensured that the criticism
would indeed be constructive and not destructive.

In contrast to Barb's fluency in the Language of Effective
Listening, Bob's interactions with Sam and his secretary reflected
almost total ignorance of proper, achievement-enhancing

communication. He allowed outside matters to preoccupy and prevent him from getting all of a key message from his secretary. He responded defensively, both verbally and nonverbally, to Sam's negative opening statements and never recovered. Then Bob bludgeoned his secretary with verbal abuse and drove her out of the company.

Both Barb and Bob had intellect, academic background, and business savvy going for them. But Bob's strengths never led to personal success because he didn't know how to listen to others effectively and speak to them in terms that would build rather than destroy bridges of understanding and friendship.

Much of success rests on the sense of self-esteem, trust, and confidence that we nurture in others. No matter what the individuals' intellectual abilities or educational backgrounds, they will never become good managers unless the boss, subordinates, and colleagues really want to work with them. Opportunities for achievement go to those whom others like and trust. To set up this kind of solid working relationship and friendship with others, you need to listen to them effectively. In short, it's essential to become fluent in the Language of Effective Listening.

Chapter Two

I Don't Want to Hear It!

For if we would judge ourselves, we should not be judged.

—St. Paul

Not many people find good listening ability coming to them naturally. Even the most personable among us often don't see the need to be effective listeners on a consistent basis. We do make the effort when we think it crucial—usually. When we have the option of listening or not listening, and the risk of missing out on something important does not seem too great, the normal tendency is to tune out as quickly as possible.

Much of this type of resistance to listening comes out of our subconscious. Our stated excuses usually run to being too busy, or to thinking that the potential value of the information to be gleaned is not all that high, or at least not worth the time it will take to absorb it.

It's one more thing to concentrate on, and I have too much on my plate already. "I don't want to hear it!"

Yes, in the hectic day in which we live, it is tough, in a way, to be a good listener. An awful lot is being thrown at us. We are the target of far more messages than was any other society in human history. Our natural response to the onslaught is to try where possible to install filters (if not solid barriers!). Deep down we worry about personal overload. And it is true that the more that is brought to our attention the less we will be able to concentrate on what is already in our minds. We all know about the spreading-yourself-too-thin syndrome. Building defense mechanisms is a logical and understandable response.

That's the way it looks from a purely personal perspective. But approaching the problem from a different angle puts a much more hopeful light on it. It's a matter of turning an arbitrarily deaf ear or—much more to your own ultimate advantage—employing a language of effective listening that builds on readily developed discernment skills. The latter keeps you from losing precious time hearing out things that will be of no use to you now or ever, yet protects you from missing out on communication that will affect you from here to eternity.

There is, unfortunately, in some circles something of a perverse stigma attached to the idea of being a good listener. It is perceived to be a passive trait, and *that* just doesn't cut it in our rough-and-tumble world.

The false premise in this kind of attitude is the idea that communication takes place only or primarily through talk. And some of us even worry that if we are not talking we are not in control, that to listen is tantamount to not being in control of the situation. The trouble is that too much talk is a turnoff. Excessive talkers should not assume that they are being heard. They may be "in control" far less than they think.

On the other hand, it's also important not to presume that being a quiet person automatically makes you a good listener. There is a lot more to effective listening than just keeping still. You cannot talk and listen at the same time. But, by the same token, silence does not guarantee that you are absorbing the message of another.

Our society virtually ignored for many years the need to learn to listen. The communications explosion of the recent past came upon us with little attention to the development of listening skills, and much of our grief today is attributable to this oversight. We owe it to each other to be good listeners. It is the basis of good relationships and mutual respect and understanding. Yet listening skills are for most of us quite a low priority. Even intelligent people caricature listening as a passive trait. As a result, we have missed out on the benefits.

A popular movie some years ago acknowledged the problem with a throwaway line, "Nobody listens to anybody anymore."

Fortunately, it is never too late to start listening properly. Acquiring the right skills just takes some concentration and perseverance. The outcome can revolutionize your communications with others—at home, at work, any place where there is verbal interaction.

The place to start is with the realization that you are communicating while you listen. Indeed, as a listener you may be able to communicate more in quality and quantity than those who are speaking. If necessary, keep repeating this principle in your mind and out loud. The bottom line is not what you say but what you communicate. An unreceived message is a wasted message. As the Language of Effective Listening is explained, your eyes may be opened to options you never knew anything about and never thought possible.

The Language of Effective Listening uses your whole body. It begins with the ear, but it mobilizes everything within you. Smiling and nodding, when right, are only the beginning. Take the challenge seriously, and you will allow listening to engage your whole being in the communications process. Think of yourself not as a helpless sponge at the mercy of the speaker but as a live bundle of energy emitting penetrating message rays in a dozen or more subtle ways, stimulating, informing, teaching, convincing, encouraging, and challenging. Think of yourself as an asset to the speaker, but one in which *mutual* enrichment is taking place. To realize the power inherent in "mere" listening is truly transformational.

To be sure, listening is sometimes regarded as a threat. Most of us have limits to our flexibility and tolerance; we reserve areas of ultimate concern in our lives that we do not wish to leave open to any kind of change. That is a human right.

Such concerns become particularly relevant in individuals or whole societies that we perceive as enemies. So be it. The real point here is that even in the most hostile encounters we have the choice of simply making noise or using the occasion to listen intelligently enough to learn. No situation is so bad that we cannot glean something of value and thus chalk up a personal gain. It may not be as momentarily gratifying as yelling insults, but in the long term it sets us ahead.

The Language of Effective Listening has surprisingly little to do with actual sound. Technically, we cannot physically shut down our ears unless we cover them in some way. With a few exceptions, such as ball players who wear ear plugs so they don't hear boos from the crowd, we frown on such measures. Cutting off the message at the brain is the preferred means of tuning out unwanted sounds.

Inasmuch as listening is so dependent on the ears, however, it's well to appreciate the astounding intricacy of these very small organs. They are a marvel of miniaturization. To study how they work is one of the most interesting scientific and anatomical adventures imaginable.

And to think that it's one of the few human organs of which we get more than one! That, along with only having one mouth, has prompted many to observe that we should listen twice as much as we talk!

It is all too obvious, but sometimes we forget about the connection between hearing and listening. Except in cases of hearing impairment, we are obliged to rely on our hearing ability to listen. Not infrequently, misunderstanding can be blamed on the failure of sound to arrive at its intended destination. Distractions may or may not be the cause. If you are not hearing clearly what is said, take whatever steps are necessary to correct the situation or compensate for it.

Another basic element you do not want to overlook is that your willingness to be a listener may not be enough to make you one in every instance. You should even consider enduring periods of silence if it helps the would-be speaker. You will realize that patience is a key ingredient in the Language of Effective Listening.

* * * * *

Immediately after the concluding workshop session, Mary took a limousine to the airport. Skeptical that she could gain something from almost anyone who spoke to her, she particularly doubted that the elderly limousine driver might offer anything of value. After all, she was a well-placed executive and had more knowledge than most people had. But she decided to ask the driver if she could sit up front and talk with him. She used all of the skill she had practiced in the workshop to try to draw him out. She asked the proper questions in the correct way and used her "power listening" skills to direct the conversation toward what seemed to be of value to her. He told his stories as she listened.

Ten days later my telephone rang, and Mary excitedly told me of what she had learned from the driver. "But," she gushed, "I didn't call you to tell you that we can learn something from almost everybody. You already know that. I had to call because a florist just came to my office with an arrangement of flowers from that limo driver. And . . ." At this point her voice broke, and she had difficulty getting out what she wanted to say. "And . . . with the flowers came this note, 'Dear Mrs. B., Thank you for giving me one of the most wonderful mornings of my life!' " Mary was learning the benefits of effective listening.

Months later Mary called again. The limousine driver had left his previous job and become the chauffeur for the vice president of an electronics firm. This firm was interested in purchasing components from Mary's company. Would Mary be interested in meeting his boss?

* * * * *

After a week of meetings in Chicago, I was very tired. I love working with the people in our training sessions, and I always try to give 110 percent to make it an enjoyable and beneficial experience for everybody. When I got my boarding pass, as usual, I requested an aisle seat with the middle seat to be left open. In the window seat was a man dressed very unlike me. I was wearing a typical, three-piece business suit. He was wearing jeans, a cowboy shirt, and boots, and he had very long hair. I was glad we were dressed so differently, because I assumed he would naturally find our dissimilar appearance sufficient reason to ignore me. He appeared to be asleep. Gratefully, I picked up my book and began to read for a few minutes. I planned to spend a few minutes reading and then sleep the rest of the trip.

I had hardly dipped into the text when he spoke. "I see you're reading my favorite book." With that comment he hooked my attention. I had to decide. Should I excuse myself and politely tell him that I was tired, was about ready to take a nap, and possibly could I chat with him later, or should I allow the conversation to continue? I knew never to feign attention. This could be an ideal time to get a good illustration for our workshops. Here was a man whom I had never met, and, in all probability, would never see again. Would he be able to tell me something of value if I gave him my undivided attention?

Tired as I was, I decided to give it a try. Turning toward him and preparing to give 100 percent attention, I responded to his statement in a way that would encourage conversation. For three hours I listened to him talk about his sales business, his singles club, and his personal aspirations. He got a "kick" out of the fact that although he barely graduated from college he was probably making twice as much as I, a college professor. His estimation was way off. He was making five times as much as I was. We both had a good laugh over that.

I was tired when the conversation began. By the end, I was completely exhausted. Worse, I had learned nothing of value for all my effort. I consoled myself as I walked down the ramp, at least it was good practice in listening when you are tired. Then I heard him call my name, "Art, wait a minute, I'd like to have your card."

I gave him a card and asked why he wanted it. He replied, "You really listened to me, and in response to something I said, you mentioned a charity in Brooklyn that you help support. I want to support that charity and will send you a check every month for the next 12 months." And, he did! We had not met before, nor have we ever had occasion to meet again. But the trust level rose so high in that encounter, he was willing to send money to a complete stranger.

* * * * *

A man left the opening workshop session determined to listen to his wife. She had refused to concede that they needed a new car. He came back to our second day of training to tell us that his wife had agreed that a car was necessary, and they had already begun their search. Why this sudden turnaround? He listened to her "arguments" about why a new car "was not necessary" and found that she was not opposed to buying a new car at all. She only wanted a chance to express her opinion, to share her view, to be heard!

* * * * *

Listening attentively is not in itself a cure-all. However, the probability is high that you will lose more insights and opportunities by *not* keeping up this listening habit as compared to the few nonproductive conversations you may have to endure. Even when no immediate payoff seems apparent, remember that you are reaping three benefits: (1) you are raising self-esteem, (2) you are developing your listening skill, and (3) you are learning and broadening your interests and vocabulary.

Listening Pays

Raises self-esteem.
Develops skills.
Broadens interests.

Chapter Three

Give Yourself
a Surprise

The unexamined life is not worth living.

—Plato

Studies over 10 years show that constructive self-examination is a beneficial step toward personal responsibility and fulfillment. People who constructively judge themselves are easier to work and live with. Associates, family, and friends have more confidence in individuals who accept responsibility for their own development.

We guide you through five proven steps of profitable self-analysis relating to your listening habits. Surprises guaranteed! Your success will depend on your motivation. Those five steps are listed below:

1. Decide who will receive the benefit of your improved listening habits. Focus on these people during your self-development period.
2. Decide which of your listening habits are nonproductive.
3. Look at your behavior to see how frequently you think you behave this way.
4. Identify what productive habits will replace the nonproductive ones.
5. Commit yourself to practicing these positive skills regularly, at least 8 times a day for 21 days.

Personal change requires motivation. To have in mind specific people with whom you would like to improve your relationship is great motivation. In the space supplied jot down the initials of five people with whom you would like to improve your communication. Choose people from your professional and personal life.

Names of Individuals with Whom I Will
Improve Communication

1. _____

2. _____

3. _____

4. _____

5. _____

TEN MOST PRACTICED
NONPRODUCTIVE LISTENING HABITS

Examine the following list of nonproductive listening habits and ask yourself how often you practice these habits when listening to the "Favored Five" people you choose from your professional and personal life. A checklist at the end will help you examine your listening habits.[1] Then you can plan what you will change and decide how to do it.

Bad Listening Habit 1: Lack of
Interest in the Subject

There are no uninteresting subjects. There are only uninterested people.

—G. K. Chesterton

Those with the widest interests are the most interesting people, the best listeners, and the most successful persons. Poor listeners have a very limited list of interests and frequently limit their professional development and personal satisfaction. Becoming interested in the subjects that interest the people you talk to has at least three benefits.

The first benefit is that you raise the self-esteem of the speaker, and that makes *you* a winner. Self-esteem is the number one prerequisite to personal productivity. By listening to the people who are important to you, you are telling them they are important to you. What they are saying is important to them. Therefore, it is important for us to listen. Think of a time in recent memory that you were especially affected by someone listening to you. Or remember how you felt as a child when someone really listened to you.

Agape has the most profound meaning of the several Koine Greek words for love. Agape is doing for other people what they need. It is a love of doing, not merely a feeling. By acting in the best interests of the speaker, your feelings will frequently change toward that individual. But even if your feelings don't change, you will have helped the speaker and therefore helped yourself by listening.

The second benefit of paying attention is that you learn new vocabulary words indirectly. Studies show that the most successful individuals, whatever their occupation, are those with the largest vocabularies. The average-educated adults in the United States have about 2,000 words in their vocabulary and use 400 of those words in 80 percent of their conversations. The most successful people have a few hundred more words in their working vocabulary.

A reason these people are more successful than the average is that they have at their disposal a wider choice of solutions to problems. They have more hooks to hang their ideas on. We think categorically. Categories are defined by words. The larger the vocabulary, the greater the capacity for thought categories providing alternative means of identifying and resolving problems. Psycholinguists call this capacity for various solutions "requisite variety." The two most efficient means of building vocabulary and gaining requisite variety are through reading and listening.

Third, effective listeners are taught directly, too. All of us are experts in some area in which others are ignorant. All of us have our own genius. The effective listener discovers and profits not only from the style of others but also from the content of their messages. Become a constructively selfish listener. Recognize that you can get something from what a person has to say at least 80 percent of the time. Listen for what will be valuable to you. As Lyman Steil says, "Ask, 'What's in it for me?' and look for the Value Moment of Listening." Eighty percent of the time you will discover something of value.

Bad Listening Habit 2: Becoming So Preoccupied with the Package that You Miss the Content

Effective listeners recognize the speaker's unusual speech, diction, accent, dress, hairstyle, grammar, and any other idiosyncrasies, but get beyond those to gain the content of the message. Some listeners, however, are diverted by speakers who look at the floor while talking, speak in a monotone, play with objects, or wear unattractive or inappropriate clothes.

When Albert Einstein walked on the Princeton University campus to give a lecture, students noticed that he wore sneakers, high-water pants, and no socks. The bad listeners chuckled during the entire presentation and missed the message. Effective listeners got beyond his unique appearance and were enriched by the content of his speech.

Douglas Hyde was a leading member of the Communist party in Britain and news editor of the *London Daily Worker.* In 1948, he renounced the party and joined the Catholic church with his wife and children. After his political and religious conversion he wrote *Dedication and Leadership*. The chapter entitled "The Story of Jim" illustrates the importance of getting beyond the appearance to the message and the person.

Hyde ended a lecture saying that the Communist party could take anyone willing to be trained in leadership and turn him into a leader. Jim approached Hyde. Jim was very short and extremely overweight with a flabby white face, a cast in one eye, and a most distressing stutter. Here was the greatest challenge Hyde could imagine. The first step was to build self-confidence, and the second to give something to be confident about. Hyde gave Jim something to believe in, and he began to train him.

After a time, Hyde told Jim that he was ready to become a tutor of others. He trained Jim in leadership and groomed him for success as a tutor. Next Hyde forced Jim to become articulate by giving him knowledge others didn't have and insisting he express it to others. Jim's next stage of development came as a street-corner propagandist and agitator. Finally, he became a national leader of his trade union.

A listener deceived by hearing her slow speech may underestimate the acumen of one of the most intelligent individuals I have ever met in the corporate community. She suffers from Parkinson's disease, and although the motor movement of her tongue is slow, she has a legal mind with laser speed. Effective listeners get the content and avoid stumbling over delivery errors. How often are valuable insights missed because the listener judges the person or the delivery and not the content of the message?

Bad Listening Habit 3:
Interrupting the Speaker

How often have you drawn a premature conclusion and interrupted the speaker either inwardly or outwardly, then missed the point? Ultimately, you may have found that the speaker was consistent, and you were wrong. Effective listeners, even if overstimulated by what is being said, "hold their fire" until they have heard the complete message.

You don't like to be interrupted when you are talking. You want the listener to wait until you are finished, think about what was said, and then respond. Instead of interrupting and fighting for "air space," you need to be patient and give the speaker the needed time. It's just as rude to step on peoples' ideas as it is to step on their toes.

Bad Listening Habit 4: Focusing on Details and Missing the Point

Poor listeners, like "Dragnet's" Sergeant Friday, listen only for the facts. Focus solely on the details, and you may miss the point. Effective listeners identify the *concept*. The concept is like the hub of a wheel; the facts are the spokes. If the facts are not connected to the concept when the pressure of time bears upon the wheel, the wheel becomes unbalanced and throws off the spokes. The facts are lost. We remember what we understand well. How often have you been taken literally and misunderstood?

Bad Listening Habit 5: Forcing Everything into a Preconceived Outline

Poor listeners often impose their own organizational pattern on the speaker. Effective listeners identify the speaker's outline and follow it when taking notes or thinking through the message.

Overcoming personal preconceptions helps you hear things as they are, not as you wish they were. Poor listeners often mentally edit remarks they don't like or distort meanings to avoid having to come to grips with viewpoints they resent.

ILLUSTRATION 3–1
Effective Listeners Get the Point

*Bad Listening Habit 6: Demonstrating
an Inactive Body State*

Poor listeners habitually display an inactive body state. Effective listeners recognize that their physical stance will have an influence on their ability to concentrate. They use the RELATIONS model, which we talk about in a later chapter. A sloppy posture frequently denotes an unconcerned attitude. When you adopt a positive physical stance, you automatically become more attentive. When was the last time you pretended to listen when your mind was actually miles away? If you pretend, people will see through you.

* * * * *

While daydreaming in the first grade, I was startled into reality by the teacher's voice, "Now turn in your papers, class." What had she asked us to write on the paper? My mind raced. I looked at the paper of the girl sitting next to me—hers was done and ready to be turned in. Hurriedly I copied what she had written. "Whew!" I breathed a sigh of relief. You can imagine my surprise when a few minutes later the teacher asked? "Why are there two papers for Linda and none for Arthur?" The teacher had given the instructions to put our name, address, and date at the top of the page. I had copied the name and address of the girl sitting next to me.

* * * * *

Don't fake attention. If you cannot give your full attention, postpone the important conversation.

Bad Habit 7: Creating or Tolerating Distractions

In a room where someone is speaking, there is an area that can be identified as the *cone of attraction*. It's the area in the room within the vision of the speaker, where that person gets the most attention and where the fewest distractions are encountered. Those who stand or sit outside this cone are less likely to be in touch with the speaker. (It also helps people to listen more carefully if they sit close together.)

Poor listeners believe that circumstances control their lives. In the Language of Effective Listening you take control by eliminating as many distractions as possible or by listening through distractions you cannot remove. How often do you allow the telephone to interrupt a conversation? When a conversation is interrupted, the listener forgets what was said the last few seconds even though trying to concentrate on the conversation.

ILLUSTRATION 3-2
Effective Listeners Get Rid of Distractions

Recognize and eliminate distractions. At home, people leave the television on while talking at the dinner table. With family members, you may find it helpful to set aside special times for undistracted conversation. Make a rule not to conduct telephone conversations at mealtime. At work, arrange your furniture to optimize productivity. (Note: Facing an active hallway or outer offices is seldom conducive to getting a lot of work done.) At parties, don't try to carry on more than one conversation at a time.

Bad Listening Habit 8:
Tuning Out Difficult Material

Poor listeners tune out difficult material. Good listeners work on building their own word power. They exercise their minds. They plan to listen to people, discussions, and presentations that will expand their vocabulary. The average TV program is written for a sixth-grade vocabulary. Effective listeners understand this, and although they still know how to enjoy that level of material on occasion, they seek out programs like "Nova," "Meet the Press," and others that are intellectually stimulating. Whatever your political affiliation, William Buckley will challenge you to learn new words. Individuals who continue to remain active and grow mentally can actually gain IQ points in their older years. Even after retirement your verbal intelligence can increase so that you will become a more productive and valuable person to yourself and to the economy, as well as to your family and friends.

Our ears need practice for more difficult listening situations. When either listening or reading, remember words you don't know and look them up.

Consider also that you don't have to understand all the words in a sentence to recognize meaning. Too often we bail out of conversations when, with a little effort, we could understand what is being said.

Here are simple, familiar thoughts expressed in unfamiliar terminology. How many "obfuscations of celebrated oracular utterances" can you figure out?

1. Scintillate, scintillate, asteroid minific.
2. Members of an avian species of identical plumage congregate.
3. Surveillance should precede saltation.
4. Pulchritude possesses a solely cutaneous profundity.
5. It is fruitless to become lachrymose over precipitately departed lacteal fluid.
6. Freedom from encrustations of grime is contiguous to rectitude.
7. Eschew the implement of correction and vitiate the scion.
8. It is fruitless to attempt to indoctrinate a superannuated canine with innovative maneuvers.

9. The temperature of aqueous content of an unremittingly ogled saucepan does not reach 212 degrees F.
10. All articles that coruscate with resplendence are not truly auriferous.

* * * * *

Answers: 1. Twinkle, twinkle little star. 2. Birds of a feather flock together. 3. Look before you leap. 4. Beauty is only skin deep. 5. Don't cry over spilled milk. 6. Cleanliness is next to godliness. 7. Spare the rod and spoil the child. 8. You can't teach an old dog new tricks. 9. A watched pot never boils. 10. All that glitters is not gold.

Bad Listening Habit 9: Letting Emotions Block the Message

Emotions are wonderful and important. They bring color, meaning, and purpose to our lives. Emotionally laden words can give great satisfaction or arouse personal antagonism. Anyone who knows more about what touches our emotions than we do is in a position to control us. Millions of dollars are spent every year to find ways to control us through triggering our emotions. When emotions go up, rationality goes down.

In some of our workshops we used tape recordings of very emotional topics such as Right To Life versus Freedom of Choice. Different voices present the pro and the con sides of the issues, but the same statistics are used by both presenters. After listening to the tapes the participants are asked ten questions about what was said.

Following the presentation of one side of the argument, a man came forward and requested a copy of the tape so that he might disprove the statistics that were presented. I tried to tell him that both sides of the tape contained the same statistics. It was the nonverbal communication, not the data, that made the difference. He was so emotionally aroused he could not hear me! We cannot win an argument much less gain a hearing without hearing the other side. Emotional control makes hearing possible.

On a long drive I tuned my car radio to a talk show that held views diametrically opposed to mine. Within seconds of hearing the subject discussed, I sensed the bias in the speaker and found my emotions going through the roof. But I gained emotional control and forced myself to listen. Guess what? I learned something. "Those" people did know something that I didn't. If we identify what touches our emotions and then practice control, we can gain emotional control.

Bad Listening Habit 10: Daydreaming

Good listeners take advantage of the fact that they think seven to ten times faster than anyone can talk. They use this advantage of thought speed to process the message—to evaluate, to review, to anticipate, and to summarize the message the speaker is sending. They look for the purpose and for key words and concepts. They discern the overt and subliminal outline of the message. They recognize the significance of the emotional content and attitude as well as the conceptual and verbal content. They are aware that more than 700,000 nonverbal cues are being sent toward them. Through concentration and the exercise of certain techniques, they are able to learn more about what the speaker is saying than the speaker often intended to convey. The use of tape players with variable speed control proves that the average adult can listen to 282 words per minute with no loss in comprehension, yet the average person speaks at only about 150 words per minute.

SELF-ASSESSMENT

Now take a moment to examine yourself according to the
criteria explained above. Think again of the Favored Five
with whom you desire to improve your relationship during
the next 30 days. Indicate which idea most closely describes
your listening habits: Almost always, Usually, Sometimes,
Seldom, or Almost never.

The national average is 62.[2] Your associates and friends
may or may not agree with you. One way to get a compari-
son of your perception with their perception of your listening behavior is to use our confidential, positively oriented
computerized listening inventory.

Now, in the first column below, again list the initials of
the Favored Five, those people with whom you want to
enhance your communication. In the next column write the
habit you want to eliminate and its number in the third
column.

	Person	Habit (Negative statement)	Number of Habit
a.			
b.			
c.			
d.			
e.			

TABLE 3-1
Checklist of Bad Listening Habits

Listening Habit	Almost Always	Usually	Some-times	Seldom	Almost Never	Initials
1. Lack of interest in the subject						
2. Becoming so preoccupied with the package that you miss the content						
3. Interrupting the speaker						
4. Focusing on details and missing the point.						
5. Forcing everything into a preconceived outline						
6. Demonstrating an inactive body state						
7. Creating or tolerating distractions						
8. Tuning out difficult material						
9. Letting emotions block the message						
10. Daydreaming						
Total Score						

Score Key: Almost always = 2 Usually = 4 Sometimes = 6 Seldom = 8 Almost never = 10

Don't Forget to Listen to Yourself, Too!

He was the receivers' coach for the New York Giants football team, going through one of the worst seasons in the team's history. On an average, professional football coaches last fewer than three years with a team.[3] At the end of this particular season, all the offensive coaches were fired. For Ted Plumb, it was one of the worst years of his life.

Ted was hired by another club where, driven by his character and intelligence, he applied what he learned that year with the Giants. This subsequently enabled him to help the Chicago Bears win a Super Bowl. He says that he took one step backward to take two steps forward. He took a good look at himself and learned from earlier mistakes. Mistakes are stepping stones to success if we are willing to learn from them. Some Japanese companies require their employees to admit to a certain number of mistakes each year. Our human tendency is to deny the wrongs we commit. The smartest among us face up to mistakes and learn from them.

Count the cost! Is it worth the effort to learn a new habit that will build better relationships? Even if you fail in some of your attempts to improve?

Turn your trials into triumphs! Compare the list of skills below with the list of habits from the previous page. Those negative habits are restated below as positive skills. Circle the skills below that correspond to the habits you plan to change.

Listening Skills

1. Listen for something of value in whatever the person is saying. Raise that person's self-esteem.
2. Judge the content of the message, not the deliverer or the delivery of the message.
3. Use "active silence." Remain silent and listen until the person is finished speaking. Think about what was said. Pause, then respond.
4. Get past the details to the real point.
5. Synchronize with the speaker's verbal and nonverbal communication.

6. Adopt an active body state: lean toward the person in an alert body position.

7. Control or eliminate distractions.

8. Concentrate on unfamiliar material and stretch your mind.

9. Practice emotional control.

10. Take advantage of thought speed: put on your EARS (Evaluate, Anticipate, Review, & Summarize) while the person is talking. Listen for key words and look for nonverbal messages.

Now write the initials of the same five people with whom you will build more effective communication. In the right column write down the listening skills that you want to develop with each person. Restate in your own words. Bad habit and positive skill (good habit) numbers correspond.

Person (same initials as p. 17)	Skill Number	Habit (positive statement, same as p. 17)
a.		
b.		
c.		
d.		
e.		

Make The Commitment/Sign Your Contract

Signify that you are making the commitment to improve the communication relationship with the five people you have named by signing your name. Make the commitment now.

Name: _____ Date: _____

Visualize Your Success Now

As a senior at U.C.L.A., I had the privilege of teaching students in the psychology clinic how to improve their reading skills. Junior and senior high school students from around the country increased their reading grade level by two or three years in just eight weeks of training. This tremendous growth was made possible by a special program that incorporated as many senses as possible in the learning process.

We find, for example, that you are more likely to be successful in your attempts to learn a new positive skill if you write out what you are going to do, read it to yourself, put yourself in a relaxed mode, and see yourself doing it. The following exercise applies the technique to your desire to be a better listener.

To begin the visualization process, you must be able to relax. As you guide yourself through this exercise, you will learn how to control yourself in a new way. Prepare for the visualization exercise by asking yourself:

Whom will I listen to?

What will that person look and sound like?

Which listening skills will I use?

Where will I be listening to that person?

When will this take place?

How do I want to feel when listening to this person?

Other suggestions to help your visualization experience be more successful include the following:

1. Choose a time and place when and where you will not be interrupted.

2. Play soft music on the radio or stereo. Classical music at about 60 beats per minute works particularly well, perhaps because 60 beats per minute is about the average heart rate for a person in a relaxed mode.

3.   The more relaxed you are the more effective will be the exercise. Many people find help by listening to a brief recording of their own voice suggesting relaxation.

Place both your feet on the floor, sit up in your chair, close your eyes, and slowly inhale and exhale 10 times. When you sense that you are sufficiently relaxed look for the person in your imagination; try to see the face. Try to hear the voice of the one you are imaging. Try to create the kind of feeling you would like to have when listening to that person. Imagine yourself raising the self esteem of the person by using effective listening skills. Use the skills you decided to use during the next 30 days. Change the picture, the sounds, and the feelings until they are just what you want. Then imagine the conversation for a couple of minutes and draw it to an appropriate close.

Practice this exercise often and reap the rewards!

Five Steps to Self-Development

Decide who will benefit from your improved listening habits.
Decide which of your listening habits are not productive.
Look at your behavior to see how often you act this way.
Identify what productive habits will replace those that do not produce.
Commit yourself to practice these positive skills regularly.

Chapter Four

Success with Challenge Number One

Communication is everything. Task performance—and life for that matter—are simply by-products of communication patterns.[1]

—Tom Peters

In his book *Celebration of Life,* the sociobiologist Rene Dubos looks behind a growing dilemma in our world. "The most distressing aspect of the modern world is not the gravity of its problem. There have been worse problems in the past. It is the dampening of the human spirit that causes many people, especially in countries of Western civilization, to lose their pride in being human and to doubt that we will be able to cope with our problems and those of the future."[2] The greatest challenge we face today may be our need to recover hope.

No one is more aware of the value of listening than diplomats, conciliators, negotiators, and arbitrators. Many of them can do it well. Unfortunately, political considerations repeatedly prevent these experts from extracting the full potential of hope that may reside in given situations and that their abilities could produce.

Loss of hope is often manifested as depression. "Depression, which is often related to low self-esteem, costs the United States of America $5 billion a year in direct drug and hospital costs."[3] We do not know the indirect cost to our country in broken families, alcoholism, drug addiction, and poor business.

When you esteem yourself you are more likely to do a better job. Untapped creative power is unleashed. You are open to positive change and welcome the challenge of new opportunities. You are more open to others, more honest in your dealings, and more likely to be supportive of your company, community, country, faith, and home. Self-esteem lies at the root of moral and ethical sensitivity. To esteem oneself is to lay the groundwork for more successful interpersonal relationships. Furthermore, a person with self-esteem is less likely to develop a chemical addiction. When you esteem yourself you build a strong sense of family, are more involved in social and political activities, and are generous to the less fortunate.[4]

As an added bonus, when you place proper value on yourself, those around you are infected with the same positive virus. What you think of yourself is more important than what others think of you. What you think of yourself will be reflected back to you in the attitudes and actions of those with whom you work and live.

RAISE SELF-ESTEEM THROUGH EFFECTIVE LISTENING

Self-esteem is related to communication. A short route to self-esteem is to esteem others. To receive respect, show respect. Remember the old proverb, "You reap what you sow"? Listen! Listen to your associates and colleagues, your friends, and loved ones.

What people say is important to them, even if it isn't important to you. You can build their esteem and your own by learning effective listening habits. Listening is the foundation for all effective communication. When you apply the Language of Effective Listening conscientiously to your colleagues and associates you give them hope because you esteem them.

To decide how you influence your associates, relatives, and friends, give yourself this test.

Does Your Listening Build Self-Esteem?

State how often you listen in a way that produces these results.

(A) Almost always, (U) Usually, (S) Sometimes, (Sel) Seldom, (A.N.) Almost never

(   ) 1. The speaker seems to be glad to have talked with you, even if you disagree on the validity or value of what was said.

(   ) 2. The speaker knows that you understood both the thoughts and feelings of what was said.

(   ) 3. You are glad to have conversed with the person even if there was a disagreement.

(   ) 4. You know and conveyed to the speaker your understanding of what was thought and felt.

(   ) 5. Both you and the speaker seem to have more energy to devote to immediate tasks than before you listened.

EFFECTIVE LISTENING BRINGS PROFESSIONAL AND ECONOMIC BENEFITS

Among students of at least average intelligence, the correlation between a student's ability to listen and grades appears to be higher than the correlation between the IQ of the individual and that person's grades. What is true in the academic

TABLE 4–1
Why Customers Quit

1% Die
3% Move away
5% Because of other friendships
9% Because of competition
14% Product dissatisfaction
68% Attitude of indifference toward a customer by some employee

---

community is true in the business world as well. *Individuals who have gone the furthest in their profession are characteristically those who are better listeners.* These achievers also have a wide range of interests because of their effective listening.

What are the benefits of effective listening? Greater productivity, increased understanding, increased job potential, and more operating efficiency. Add to those benefits the reduction of wasted time and materials. Time saved translates into saved dollars, energy, and productivity. A major computer company taught its staff effective listening skills and took ten million dollars in business away from a competitor in just one city. If your company employs 100 people and each one could raise listening efficiency by 10 percent, you would make significant gains in productivity. Thinking like that promotes real hope.

Research statistics identified why customers quit buying from a company. As Table 4–1 shows, 68 percent abandoned the supplier because of an attitude of indifference toward a customer by some employee. Effectively listening to customers and clients goes a long way toward showing customers an attitude of concern instead of indifference.

TABLE 4–2
Most Frequently Stated Reasons For Divorce

Ineffective communication
Money problems
Problems with the children
Sexual problems

EFFECTIVE LISTENING IMPROVES MARRIAGE AND FAMILY LIFE

More than 90 percent of the managers and professionals in our effective listening workshops were more interested in improving communication at home than at work. Divorce statistics disguise the widespread desire for harmonious, satisfying relationships at home. If effective communication increases productivity and satisfaction on a job that will end in retirement, what might it do for relationships you want to last a lifetime?

In marriage, the ability to negotiate differences is the greatest predictor of success. Effective negotiation requires effective listening. Of the four most frequently stated reasons for divorce, couples cited poor communication as the number one problem. Each of the other three most frequently stated reasons are all related to communication. See Table 4–2.

Money problems not only spring from lack of funds, but also from the question of "how do we spend what we have?" That is a communication problem. Problems with children have roots in disagreement on how to deal with the children, also a communication problem. Similarly, most sexual problems are due to communication difficulties. A sexual relationship involves communicating on many different levels. Ineffective communication will result in sexual dysfunction.

"Seeing yourself through your partner's eyes could work wonders," suggests Samuel Schreiner, Jr. in his article, "A Question That Can Save Marriages." Schreiner asks couples to ask themselves, *"What* is it like to be married to me?" As you answer this question you get your partner's mindset and see, hear, and feel as your spouse would. You listen to yourself as you perceive your partner to be listening. Schreiner cites incidents of dramatic change that took place when spouses listened to themselves and realized how they must seem to the other.[5] Herein lies hope.

EFFECTIVE LISTENING IS GOOD FOR YOUR HEALTH!

To be human is to communicate—to talk, listen, and respond to other human beings. But this constant dialogue has a dramatic effect on our bodies, especially on the heart and blood vessels. In his pathbreaking work, *The Language of the Heart,* Dr. James J. Lynch conclusively demonstrates for the first time how simple human dialogue dramatically affects the body's entire cardiovascular system. The familiar process of talking and listening to others has important consequences for health and well-being.

"The language of the heart," according to Dr. James J. Lynch, is much more than a poetic metaphor for thoughts and feelings we cannot name; it is a medically established reality. By continuously monitoring blood pressure and other vital signs, Lynch and his associates investigated the impact of human dialogue in hundreds of experiments and clinical settings among migraine patients and sufferers of hypertension as well as among people with normal blood pressure.

The findings astonished subjects and researchers alike. The blood pressure of every subject rose when that person spoke and went down when each listened. Even more

TABLE 4–3
Years of Life Lost Due to Hypertension[6]

	Men		Women	
Blood Pressure Level	*Age 35*	*Age 65*	*Age 35*	*Age 65*
140/90	3 years	2 years	2 years	1.5 years
160/95	6	4	4	3
180/100	8	5	5.5	4

intriguing, most of the subjects were completely oblivious of these dramatic changes. Dr. Lynch argues that this language of the heart cries out to be heard; if ignored, unanswered, or misunderstood, it can produce terrible physical suffering, even premature death.

LISTENING WELL DOESN'T COME EASY

Eighty percent of all business communications have to be repeated and seldom more than 20 percent of what top management says is understood five levels below.[7] Few people realize how much of their lives is spent listening and how badly they do it. Even fewer understand how important listening can be to them economically, socially, and for their self-fulfillment. Listening is the number one problem in managerial efficiency. The mortar and cement of business are its systems of communication.

People in business are beginning to discover that the spoken word rather than the written word is the fulcrum on which significant communication turns. The effectiveness of the spoken word may hinge not so much on how people talk as on how they listen. Poor listening skills are responsible for more breakdowns in communication and resultant loss in productivity than any other skill or management technique.

Your time is precious, yet frequently time is lost through ineffective communication and listening errors. You make plans for a dinner date tonight; your guests planned to come tomorrow. You thought your partner said Columbus, Ohio, not Columbus, Georgia, and you fly to the wrong city.

When Italian economist and sociologist Alfredo Pareto discovered that 80 percent of the wealth of Italy was in the hands of 20 percent of the people, he established the 80/20 principle. That ratio has since emerged in many contexts: that 80 percent of sales are said to be generated by 20 percent of the sales force, 80 percent of the company's profits are derived from 20 percent of its products. Even 80 percent of personal productivity arises from only 20 percent of one's skills.

By applying Pareto's 80/20 principle, Dr. Harold Smith of Brigham Young University demonstrated the importance of listening as a management tool. Smith asked 457 certified administrative managers, "Which of the many management skills are most important to success?" The twenty skills that appeared most frequently were identified and placed in random order. Then 250 certified administrative managers were asked to place the skills in order of importance. All five of the top skills were communication skills. Listening was ranked number one.[8]

According to a report in the *Harvard Business Review*, the ability to communicate is the most promotable quality an executive, manager, salesperson, or anyone can possess. Asked by the University of Michigan graduate school, "Which courses best prepare one for business leadership?" 1,158 newly promoted top executives responded with a high degree of unanimity. Business communication was the most common response with 71.4 percent rating it very important. Finance was the second highest, with 64.7 percent.[9]

Old Habits Die Hard!

In our hurry-up society where everything needs to be done yesterday, we think we don't have time to listen. We think about our own concerns or how we will respond to the person talking to us. As soon as the person is through speaking, we say what we want to say. Or, worse yet, we interrupt before the person is finished.

We could hear even before birth. Some researchers say we recognized our mother's voice in utero at six months. By the time we were born, we preferred female voices. Soon we could detect the relationship between our mother's mouth movements and the sounds we heard.[10]

As children we were frequently very attentive to what our environment said to us. Often we understood more of what our parents were saying to each other than our parents did. Listening was a survival skill.

By the time we entered first grade, we learned it was unnecessary to be attentive even when someone was speaking directly to us. This inattention became our listening style, a noncommunication skill that was maintained through school and into the business world. No one corrected us. Rarely were good listening skills required or rewarded. It's no wonder the average adult listens below a 25 percent efficiency level.

TO PROFIT FROM EFFECTIVE LISTENING YOU MUST INVEST

Internal and external stress factors prevent us from listening effectively. Past experience acts like a filter, prejudicing us to the meaning the speaker is trying to convey. As senders (speakers) and receivers (listeners), our backgrounds, educations, presuppositions, prejudices, belief systems, and

ILLUSTRATION 4–1
Average Listening Efficiency Is Poor

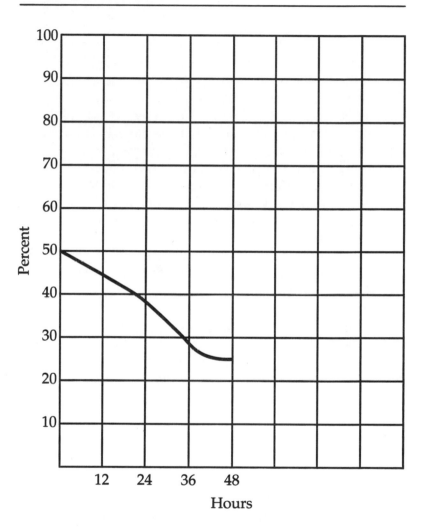

Immediately following a speech, the average listener comprehends approximately 50% of what he hears.

Within 48 hours, the comprehension level drops to 25% or less.

experiences provide mental filters through which we understand the words that we send and receive.

An unabridged English dictionary can list 450,000 or more words, but regardless of education the average person uses only 400 words in 80 percent of his or her spoken vocabulary.[11] You might think that 80 percent of our communication problem would be solved if we understood the primary meaning of those 400 words. The difficulty is that those basic 400 words have 14,500 different meanings. To further cloud the issue, language is changing so rapidly that one thousand new meanings are added to familiar vocabulary each year. With so many meanings for relatively few words, it is no wonder the message that was heard was not the message you sent. We dare not assume that because we use the same word in a conversation we mean the same thing. The word *prejudice* means to *prejudge*. We are all prejudiced.

Eugene Raudsepp of Princeton Creative Research tells the story of a zoologist walking down a busy city street with a friend amid honking horns and screeching tires. He says to his friend, "Listen to that cricket!" The friend looks at him with astonishment. "You hear a cricket in the middle of all this noise?" The zoologist takes out a coin and flips it into the air. As it clinks to the sidewalk a dozen heads turn in response. The zoologist says quietly, "We hear what we listen for."[12]

We are prone to practice selectivity. We listen with selective exposure, listening primarily to opinions that agree with our own. We evaluate by selective interpretation, tending to interpret messages the way we want to understand them, often adapting them to our own preconceptions. With selective memory we internalize the messages, remembering material that supports our own viewpoints and tending to forget the kind that does not. The assignment of meaning to a term is an internal process; meaning comes from inside us.

Many internal "noises" prevent us from hearing, let alone understanding what a person says. Physically, we may be tired, hungry, have a cold, or in some way be uncomfortable. The environment may be too hot or too cold, too humid or too dry. Our minds may be distracted by an argument we had a few minutes earlier, or we may be working on an unresolved problem. Fear may cause our minds to be closed. Listener anxiety and ego involvement tend to decrease listener comprehension.[13] Objectivity tends to increase listener comprehension. "A person's mind is like a parachute; unless it is open, it doesn't function."

How many times have you tried to listen while you were doing something else? How well can you listen while you're trying to review a report or keep an eye out for an associate whose arrival is expected. Job stress or concern with what you are going to say distracts you from effectively listening to the speaker. The average attention span of the adult brain is 12 seconds.

Noises external to the speaker and listener may also be distracting. A motor, air-conditioning, other voices, and the number one distracter, the telephone, all affect effective communication. When any noise interrupts a conversation, the last few seconds of the conversation are lost unless it is reiterated. Both parties need a moment to become reoriented and to reestablish communication after an interruption.

In addition to the internal noises in the sender and the receiver and the external noises between them, sometimes the message itself is "noisy." Messages, like words, have both denotative and connotative meanings; for example, consider the images conjured by the words *burnt dead cow* compared with *broiled steak*.

Messages have latent as well as literal meanings. You send as clear a message with your tone of voice as you do with your words. A message as simple as "Look who's here!" can be laden with sarcasm, irony, or joy. Your voice's tone, pitch, volume, and modulation are the most powerful communicators of what you think and feel. Messages, like words, have different meanings in context. Subconscious and emotional needs may influence a message. What people say may not be what they mean. When a person complains about work, it may really mean that person is not getting along at home.

As communicators, our job is to determine what the speaker means by what is said. When you understand the internal noise filters, you will improve your understanding of what others are really saying. Even the most important people in your life will use words differently than you do, and you need to hear over this internal noise.

One of the first principles in reviving hope by becoming a more effective listener is to realize that we are prejudiced. Our prejudices may lead us to make invalid assumptions about what people are saying.

We are different in our particular prejudices. The closer you are in background, education, experience, belief system, and assumptions to the speaker, the more likely it is that you will understand each other. The closer you are genetically to the speaker, the more likely it is that you will effectively communicate. Trust also plays a key role.

A key hurdle en route to better communications is the recognition that you have prejudices that lead you to false assumptions. Another hurdle is to identify those prejudices. Accents, hair styles, and clothes predispose or prejudice us in a particular way. Our prejudgments need not become a roadblock to communication. Once you identify your biases, plan to do something about them. Your best strategy is to withhold judgment until you are sure of the message being sent. Don't assume the person understands or that you understand. Remember, hope is on the line!

Training of Listeners Neglected

From the ancient philosophers to now, primary emphasis in communication training has been on writing and speaking. Close to $200 billion is spent every year in education in the

United States with almost no money spent on listening training. Yet 57 percent of a grammar school student's time is spent in a listening mode; 53 percent of a high school student's time is spent in a listening mode; 69 percent of a college student's time is spent in a listening mode.[14] Over 50 percent of managers' and supervisors' work time is spent listening. Eighty-five percent of Fortune 500 companies have listening training programs on tape. But less than 15 percent actively use them.

If you are to be trained in the vital area of communication, you will likely have to train yourself. Great! Taking responsibility for your own communication training is healthy and gratifying. A study done by the University of California revealed that the happiest and best-adjusted adults were those who took responsibility for themselves.[15]

When asked, "Who is most responsible for effective communication, the speaker or the listener?" most workshop participants respond that the speaker is most responsible. The speaker chooses the subject, the context, and other variables. The listener, it is assumed, is passive. Such an assumption is a critical mistake. Sometimes, the speaker has something of value to say but communicates poorly. If the listener allows the speaker to have all responsibility for communication, the listener loses out. Who robs the listener of vital information, the speaker who had poor communication patterns, or the listener who refused to take responsibility to clarify the message?

Accept the 51 Percent Responsibility Challenge[16]

Accept the challenge to be responsible for at least 51 percent of the understanding of all communication in your life, whether you are the listener or the speaker. You will be glad you did. As Dr. Lyman Steil says, "Don't buy it, just try it. If it doesn't work, let us know." If you accept the challenge, then this book will be a significant vehicle that will enable you to profit from effective listening.

ILLUSTRATION 4–2
Percentage of Time Spent in Listening

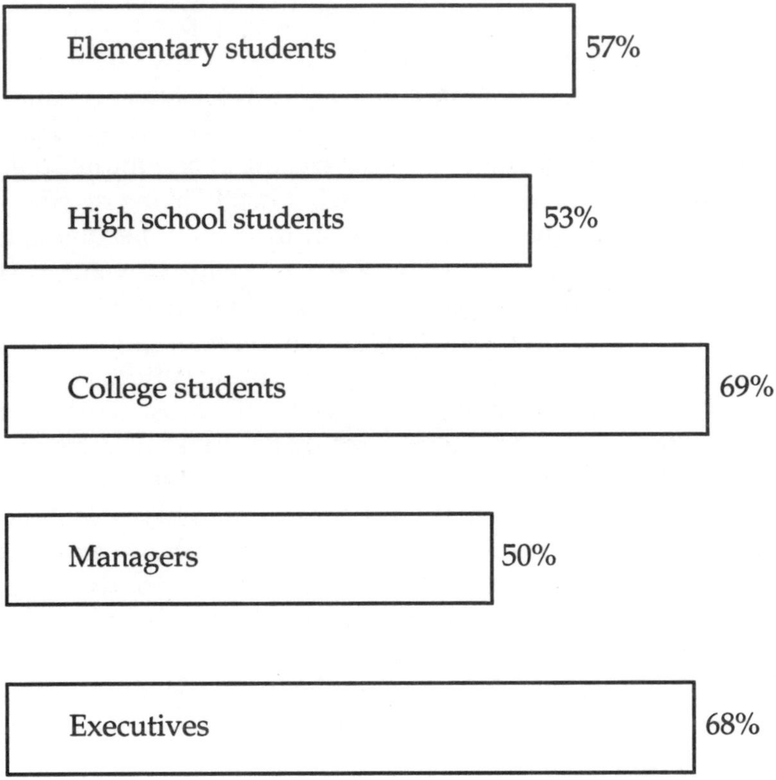

| Elementary students | 57% |

| High school students | 53% |

| College students | 69% |

| Managers | 50% |

| Executives | 68% |

OBJECTIVES DETERMINE OUTCOMES

"If you don't know where you're going, you may end up somewhere else," said Yogi Berra when he was with the New York Yankees. We might say, "If you don't know where you are going, any road will get you there."

One of our great women swimmers wanted to be the first woman to swim the channel between Catalina Island and the coast of California. She had already swum across the

English Channel in both directions. July fourth would be a historic event. Unusually cold and foggy conditions and shark-infested water made the swim more difficult. Riflemen sat on the bow of the two boats to escort her and ward off any sharks that came too close. She swam for more than 16 hours. Her mother and brother in one of the boats encouraged her on. Only a half mile from shore she dragged herself out of the water. With TV cameras focused on her she answered the question, "Why did you stop so close to your goal? Was the water too cold? Were you afraid of the sharks or too tired?"

"No," she responded. She went on to explain that she could not see the shore through the fog. Swimming for hours without seeing the shore is very difficult. Before long this great lady attempted the swim again. This time she broke the men's record in the process. Her experience illustrates Aristotle's maxim, "We stand a greater chance of hitting the target if we can see it."

Without objectives we are like the man who went up to the airline ticket counter and asked for a ticket. "What is your destination?" the agent inquired. "Oh, anywhere will do," the man responded. If you don't know where you are going, you might end up where you don't want to be. We all must establish goals that are worthy of us as human beings!

In *Man's Search For Meaning,* Viktor E. Frankl described his three years at Auschwitz and other Nazi prisons. Some of the men in the camps simply willed themselves to die. Others, who were able to sustain hope, actually grew in character. Frankl emphasizes in his logotherapy that a sufficient reason *why* you need to accomplish or reach a goal will always produce the means as to *how* you can do it!

Survivors in the prison camp were those who were willing to give up immediate satisfaction, even in a small way, for a greater future goal. A crust of stale bread might alleviate immediate hunger pangs but provide less nourishment than the rancid soup. The survivors chose the rancid soup that did not alleviate hunger but provided some nourishment in exchange for the more satisfying but less life-giving bread. The common denominator among survivors was that each had a compelling reason to live. They must survive the camp to tell the world about the living hell. Some were determined to be reunited with family. Others felt they must write a book or perform in a concert. All had reasons for surviving that were bigger than themselves and greater than their circumstances.

Objectives determine outcomes. You accomplish that for which you aim. A servo system in the brain called the reticular activating system directs you toward that which you concentrate on. The system is automatic and works like a guided missile system.

Our Objectives for You

Our three general objectives for our readers are:

1. To enable you to assess yourself and establish some specific goals.
2. To give you insight into the cost of poor listening and the benefits of effective listening.
3. To give you insight into the nature of listening as a crucial element in the communication process.

You can accomplish your objectives if you are motivated to take ownership of the learning process. Identify five people in your professional or personal life with whom you would like to enhance your relationship. We guarantee that you will build mutual trust, understanding, and confidence with those people if you apply the principles that will unfold to you.

On a separate sheet of paper jot the initials of the Favored Five people with whom you would like to develop your relationship during the next 30 days. As you read this book, think of these five and ask yourself how this material applies to your communication with them. To think about the people and principles and plan how to apply them will enable you to profit from this most important communication skill.

Chapter Five

Your Stake in the Speaker's Bottom Line

One learns people through the heart, not the eyes or the intellect.

—Mark Twain

Every conversation has a reason. Every statement has a purpose. The impetus for the conversation may be conscious or unconscious to the speaker, but the effective listener tries to discern the purpose of an individual's communication. Then the effective listener gears a response to what that purpose seems to be. For example, any father of a teenager knows the question, "Dad, is there gas in the car?" usually means, "Can I borrow the car?"

You need to be quick on your listening feet, because the purpose of a conversation can change moment by moment. As the purpose changes, effective listeners change the way in which they respond.

To be sure, figuring out the purpose is not always a piece of cake, and the speaker may not even be willing to divulge it. But stick out all your antennae and, if necessary, take a cautious guess.

PHATIC COMMUNICATION

Dr. Lyman Steil has suggested four purposes of communication.[1] The first and most often used purpose of communication is small talk, or *Phatic* communication. Small talk is often regarded as trivial or even a waste of time, but it is the kind of communication that builds binding relationships. Casual chitchat is important and requires a particular listening attitude and behavior. Phatic communication not only helps develop binding relationships but also contributes to all higher level communication purposes. Without this phatic relationship, other forms of communication become difficult and sometimes ineffective. We all have heard this:

"We've worked together on and off for six years, but I never got to know him."

"I find it very hard to talk to her."

"He's a cold fish. I respect his abilities, but I'd rather not work with him."

"I can't seem to reach that guy. He never pays any attention to us unless he wants something."

In most work environments, two extremes are found. At one end of the phatic continuum is what Dr. Steil calls the (W)acky (E)xcessive (S)mall (T)alker, Fred "Gotta Minute."[2] Whenever you see Fred, he asks, "Have you got a minute?" And he will take a few minutes to tell you about last night's mashed potatoes.

The other extreme is John "Gotta Go." He is the (E)xcessive (A)voider of (S)mall (T)alk.[3] No matter what you ask John, if it isn't directly related to his business goals, he does not have time for an answer. No binding relationships develop with people around him. His wife gives birth to twin girls, and you ask him about them. His response is, "Everything's fine—gotta go." His brother is promoted to the presidency of a major corporation; you mention this to him. "That's right—gotta go."

Interestingly, though, Fred "Gotta Minute" always seems to be late finishing his reports, late coming to meetings, late fulfilling his formal responsibilities. On the other hand, John "Gotta Go" is always punctual with his reports, always on time for meetings, and dependable in fulfilling responsibilities.

John is highly structured and goal-oriented. However, no one really gets to know him, and he doesn't know anybody. He is not bound together with the people he works with. His responses lack a certain amount of loyalty. On the other hand, Fred has a real team spirit. When the chips are down and you face a critical situation, John will ignore it because it is inconvenient, but Fred will stay up all night and work on a problem if it helps the team.

The most effective communicators are on the continuum somewhere between chatty Fred and all-business John. Small talk serves a purpose in the business community. Through casual chitchat we learn to recognize the prejudices of those with whom we work. Chewing the fat helps us understand people better. As others sense the growing understanding, they are encouraged in their attitudes toward their work. The "right dose" of small talk builds team spirit, binds relationships, and increases productivity.

A woman explained in a public workshop several years ago her discovery of the value of casual, informal conversation. She had been promoted to the position of supervisor of a pool of typists. When she first took the position, she thought she needed to get to know the people with whom she would be working. So she arrived at work thirty minutes early, set out coffee and coffee cake, and tried to get to know her people. Within six months of her becoming supervisor the productivity of that typing pool moved from fifth highest to number one.

Her practice of arriving early for small talk and coffee continued until after a particularly late evening of work she overslept. She rushed to the office, fearful that her people would be very disappointed at not having their coffee ready. Imagine the pleasant surprise upon arrival to discover that one of her people had done her job for her. That's teamwork. After some reflection, she decided that she was no longer a necessary participant. Suddenly she had gained an extra half hour in the day.

For the next year and a half she skipped the thirty minute coffee time. Then one day she showed up in a listening workshop. During the discussion about phatic communication the light of recognition shone in her eyes. With the enthusiasm of discovery she shared with the instructor what she thought was the solution to an important problem she faced on her job. The productivity of her organization had dropped from number one to number five within six months of dropping the coffee time. With the importance of phatic communication newly underscored, she decided to give the early morning coffee time priority.

Many of the people who had been a part of her pool when she first became supervisor had moved to other positions. She did not really know the individuals who had replaced them in her organization and had lost touch with those with whom she had enjoyed good communication. Six months later, after rejoining the coffee klatch, she called the instructor to report that her organization was back in the number one position.

A major corporation in the Midwest decided to increase phatic communication among employees. They did it simply and effectively by increasing the size of the tables in the lunchroom. No longer would it be possible for only three people to sit alone at lunch or coffee break. By necessity, people were brought together. Phatic communication grew, and with its growth team spirit and productivity increased.

When someone approaching you asks, "How are you?" that person is not interested in a 45-minute dissertation about your lumbago. Yet that simple question in phatic communication is a thread of communication being sent to you. To ignore the comment is to break the thread. Many threads build strong ropes.

Keep in mind, a breakdown in communication is only a broken thread. Just as a broken thread is not a broken rope, a single breakdown in communication is not a broken relationship. Only when a relationship is hanging on by a thread is the breakdown in communication dangerous.

Strong relationships build greater productivity as a listener learns to recognize when a person is engaging in phatic communication. You can be *nonjudgmental* even if you don't agree with the person. Recognize that the speaker is trying to build a relationship. You may not be interested in scuba diving or hunting or gourmet cooking, but withhold judgment at this stage. Try to understand the speaker's presuppositions, background, experiences. The best and least expensive way to show respect is to listen and try to understand that person. Say to yourself, "I have two minutes, and I'm going to give that person my full attention and respect."

Even a brief encounter that is fully focused on the speaker raises the self-esteem so crucial to raising productivity.

How to Develop Phatic Communication

Everyone, at some time in a career works with a John or Jane Gotta Go. We are frustrated in our attempts to get to know them. It can be done with the help of these useful hints.

1. Become aware of what interests the person. Then, you may be able to talk briefly about those interests and begin to develop a phatic relationship. Observe the style of clothing, car, jewelry, and office accessories this person has. Are there any pictures in the person's office? Any books or magazines? These are all conversational clues to how you may engage the person momentarily.

2. When is this person most likely to invest in a moment of phatic communication? Before work, break time, lunch, after work?

3. Where is this person most likely to invest in a moment of phatic communication? A planned meeting or even a chance meeting at an "off site" may be best. Old habits die hard. If the person characteristically does not talk at work, it will be much easier to converse at another location.

Improving phatic communication at home can be even more difficult than at work. You can successfully apply the three points above to family and friends as well as to professional colleagues. Make a breakfast date instead of a dinner date with your spouse and go to a new restaurant. Make a date with each of your children individually to eat at a new location. Follow the above suggestions and be ready to *listen*. At one time or another everybody needs and wants somebody to listen to them.

How to Limit Phatic Communication

We all know what it is like to try to get a Fred or Frieda Gotta Minute to stop talking. We don't want to be rude, but we don't want to waste time, either.

1. Recognize who the Gotta Minutes are, and prepare yourself to limit the conversation.

2. Listen intently for two minutes or whatever amount of time you decide is right.

3. Restate what Gotta Minute said in your own words so that person knows you understood the conversation. Then say that you must now move on to another task. If Gotta Minute persists, make an appointment for a later date. Set the time and place.

These principles almost always work to perfection. Both the esteem of the speaker and the valuable time of the listener are protected, and a relationship grows.

Self-Assessment Exercise

Do you have enough phatic communication with the important people in your personal and professional life? Do you need to limit phatic communication with others in your professional or personal life? In the space below, jot down the initials of important people in your personal and professional life. (These may overlap with your Favored Five.)

Professional life: _____   _____   _____

Personal life: _____   _____   _____

Now go back and put a plus sign by the initials of those with whom you want to increase your phatic communication and a minus sign by those with whom you want to reduce your phatic communication. Think about when, where, and how you will do this.

CATHARSIS

An official who must listen to the pleas of his clients should listen patiently and without rancor, because a petitioner wants attention to what he says even more than the accomplishing of that for which he came.

Ptahhotep, Egyptian Pharaoh, 1000 B.C.

A second purpose for communication is catharsis. The word *catharsis* comes from the Latin word meaning "to cleanse." Literally, catharsis is cleansing. The terms we use when we speak of catharsis are expressive of the act—get it off your chest, purge, let off steam, release emotions, vent feelings, dump your bucket. Catharsis is emotional. Be aware that when emotions go up, rationality goes down.

Catharsis can be either positive or negative in content, but emotions are strong on this level. If a person does not express these feelings, that person will interpret all communication sent through the internal filter of the emotional experience. Both the purpose of catharsis and the way in which the effective listener responds are different from phatic communication.

A man who won the lottery attended one of our workshops. From the moment he walked into the room it was quite obvious that something was on his mind. Not until he had shared the news with the group was he able to concentrate on the business at hand. Others have come into our sessions with their minds distracted by news they had just heard on the car radio or by other disquieting experiences. Until these issues "get out," the internal noise is so loud that it is hard to concentrate objectively on what anyone else is saying.

Studies have shown that when people are invited to "unload," 4 percent will physically accost you. Sixteen percent will psychologically assault you: "Keep your blanketyblank proboscis out of my business." Eighty percent will dump their bucket.

We have all been in a public place, a conveyance, or a restaurant when a total stranger went into catharsis. In such situations of anonymity people sometimes think, "I'll never see this person again so I have nothing to lose. I'll tell that person what is bothering me."

As you listen to catharsis, try to understand the *feelings* the person is expressing. The conceptual content is not nearly as important as the feelings. Try to empathize. If you focus only on the actual words that are spoken but don't listen for the deeper feelings, you may miss a lot. Effective listening gets behind the words to try to understand the deeper and often unexpressed feelings and meanings.

The challenge in listening to catharsis is not only to understand the speaker's feelings but also, in a way that is understandable to the speaker, to try to reflect back to the speaker that you do understand!

Try to reflect the speaker's physical position and gestures without giving the person the impression that you're being a mimic. If you're sincere about this, you begin to take on some of the physical characteristics of the person. This action will enhance your ability to understand the person's emotions and to reflect them back in an understandable manner.

The speaker wants *empathy*, not necessarily the solution to the problem. Impatience, anger, or irrelevant cheerfulness during cathartic venting could be disastrous to a relationship. Catharsis requires a caring, empathic, nonjudgmental listener. After you have identified with the person, understood, and reflected back how the person feels, sometimes you may be able to lead the speaker to a more objective state.

If a person never goes through catharsis, the emotional problem may become a prejudiced filter through which everything else is seen, felt, and heard as long as the hurt or other feeling is there. Cathartic fulfillment is necessary for optimal success at all other levels of communication. Effective listeners are open to give and receive catharsis.

Have you considered for whom you should be providing catharsis? Almost everyone at some time needs to communicate in this way to relieve tension. To whom can you safely let off steam? Out of the pool of those with whom you have phatic communication, usually you can find people you can trust who will be suitable individuals to receive your catharsis.

Exercise caution in choosing the person to assist you in catharsis. More than once, a career has been ruined when a professional let off steam to the wrong individual, and was misinterpreted. If you dump on the wrong desk, you're in trouble.

The best people with whom to share are those with whom you have phatic communication and know you can trust. In phatic communication, cautiously share significant tidbits and learn whom you can trust with them. Trust grows slowly and mutually. People who share feelings with you are often expressing trust in you. Even angry communication is an expression of trust in you as they reveal their feelings.

How to Develop Cathartic Communication

People who share their feelings with you will trust you to share your ideas with them.

1.   Become known as one who keeps confidential information confidential!

2.   Practice understanding how people feel when speaking with you and reflecting back this understanding.

3.   Share your honest feelings in a straightforward manner with those you can trust.

Hints on How to Limit Cathartic Communication

Often managers and others say that they listen to too much catharsis. They find it is hard to turn off a conversation saturated with feelings when they have other important work to do. This is a good problem to have but a problem nevertheless. These suggestions may help:

1.   Express your appreciation to the person for sharing the feelings with you. If the person is very emotional, you may have to say it several times before you are heard.

2.   Reiterate or paraphrase the person's last statement using the speaker's tone of voice, rate of speech, volume, pitch, and gestures. Do this two or three times if necessary to make sure the person has understood what you have said.

3.   Tell the person that you would be glad to talk some more about this subject at a specific time and place that will be better. Let the speaker know that you now have to get back to a given task. By giving the person a specific time and

place to hang on to, it is easier for the speaker to disengage from the conversation.

Self-Assessment Exercise

Do you have enough cathartic communication with the important people in your personal and professional life? Do you need to limit cathartic communication with others in your personal or professional life? In the space below, again jot the initials of important people in your personal and professional life.

Professional life: _____ _____ _____

Personal life: _____ _____ _____

Now put a plus sign by the initials of those with whom you want to increase your cathartic communication. Think about when, where, and how you will do this.

INFORMATIONAL COMMUNICATION

Two other basic purposes of communication require that the listener be more critical. A major part of the communication that you receive will be for giving information. Now you need to *be judgmental!*

Three criteria have been suggested by philosophers to help us judge the accuracy of information:

1. Is the information rationally coherent? Does the information fit into the rest of life as you understand it? Rational coherence is an essential ingredient in evaluating

information, but it is not an exclusive ingredient. You can start with the wrong assumption and still be rationally coherent.

2. The second criteria in judging information is, "Is it factually valid?" This is the test of science. If this same event were to be replicated in the same fashion again and again, would the results be the same?

3. The third criteria is logical consistency. If $1 + 1 = 2$, and $2 + 2 = 4$ then $1 + 1 + 1 + 1 = 4$. However, if the assumption is wrong in the beginning, the conclusion will be wrong. For example, to say that $2 + 2 = 5$, $3 + 3 = 7$, $4 + 4 = 9$, and $5 + 5 = 11$ is a perfectly logical statement, but it is wrong because it begins with a false assumption.

We need to hang on to whatever is valid and let go of everything that isn't. We need roots to ground us and wings to rise to new vistas. Our criteria for judgment boils down to common sense. No one is assured of perfect understanding, accuracy, and response.

LISTENING TO PERSUASION

As critical as you must be of the information that is generally received, you must be more critical of the attempts to persuade. Persuasive communication tries to (1) reinforce existing attitudes and beliefs, (2) instill new attitudes and beliefs, or (3) affect behaviors and actions. Listening to persuasion is such an important and broad issue for the listener we dedicate an entire chapter to it.

COMMUNICATIONS BONUS:
THAT'S ENTERTAINMENT!

A fifth purpose for communication is to entertain. This communication includes some of the arts and much literature, as well as sports and all forms of humor. The multifaceted light side is one of life's necessities. Those of us who have become workaholics or have no time to read purely for pleasure, see a show, laugh at jokes, or exchange pleasantries with others have shut ourselves off from many of the deepest joys and most profound experiences of life.

ILLUSTRATION 5–1
Four Basic Purposes of Communication

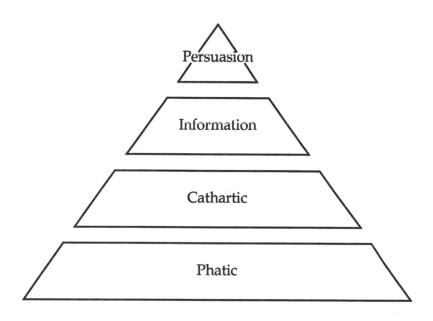

This exercise illustrates how the four basic purposes of communication can be found in a typical five-minute conversation. It is transcribed from a conversation at a Fortune 500 company.[4] The conversation has been divided into paragraphs. Read through the conversation and follow these instructions:

Place a *P* after any paragraph that is primarily *Phatic* communication.

Place a C after any paragraph that is primarily *Cathartic* communication.

Place an *I* after any paragraph that is primarily *Informational* communication.

And place a *PS* after any paragraph that is primarily *Persuasive* communication.

Setting. An office, one person is sitting at a desk working; another enters.

1. Tom [Seated].

Hi, Cathy. Good morning.

Cathy.

Good morning. How's everything?

Tom.

Good.

Cathy.

How's your son? I understand he was in an accident.

Tom.

Fine. He was very lucky. We thought for a while that his arm was broken, but fortunately it wasn't.

Cathy.

Is he still in the hospital?

Tom.

No, he was only in for a day. Right now all he has to do is to be careful and not use the arm for a few days.

Cathy.

I'm glad to hear that.

What do you think is the overall purpose of this segment of the conversation? Phatic, Cathartic, Informational or Persuasive? _____

2. Tom.

How are things in the department?

Cathy.

A mess. I had three out today. I can't believe these people. I'm killing myself out there, and they don't even bother to show up.

Tom.

I know. It can be murder trying to run your department with key people out.

Cathy.

You know, I took Larry into my office last week and talked to him for ten minutes about at least calling in when he's going to be late. Do you know that he's been out two days without calling in.

Tom.

Did you call his house?

Cathy.

What's the use? He always comes up with some stupid excuse or other. I tell you. Sometimes I get so frustrated that I just feel like throwing in the towel. You treat 'em nice and they walk all over you. You're firm with them and they think you're Scrooge.

Tom.

Hey, Cathy. This is a tough business. I can understand your frustrations.

What do you think the basic purpose of this segment of the conversation was? _____

3. **Cathy.**

Yeah, I'm sorry about dumping on you. Listen, the reason I came in was to ask about tuition refund for a course I took.

Tom [Pulling out some papers].

Just fill these out. Be sure to include the title of the course, the college where you'll take the course, and the date the course starts.

What do you think the basic purpose of this segment of the conversation was? _____

4. **Cathy.**

Thanks. I have a bit of a problem.

Tom.

What's that?

Cathy.

Well you see, I took a management course already at a local college. Would it be all right for me to apply for credit now?

Tom.

I'm afraid not. You must have prior approval to receive tuition credit.

Cathy.

What difference does it make?

Tom.

Well, the course you took may not be the appropriate one for you to have taken.

Cathy.

But what if it was the right course to take? I checked with some other managers in my position, and they told me that they had this same course approved. I'm sure that this one is the right course for me to take.

Tom.

Well, I'm sorry, Cathy, but the procedure is to contact our office before you take the course.

Cathy.

But what difference does it make? It was the right course! I don't see why I should have to lose $400 because "that's the procedure." I can't believe this place. You try to improve yourself, and they just slap you in the face. Can't you bend the rules just this once?

Tom.

Cathy, look. I can't bend the rules. We need prior approval because we are given only a certain budget, and we can't go over it. If we let you through, this sets a precedent, and we'll go out of business here.

What do you consider the overall purpose of the last segment of this conversation to be? _____

5. **Cathy.**

That's the most ridiculous thing I have ever heard. I've worked hard in this place. I never come in late. I do my job, and this is what I get. All those people abusing the system. You pat them on the back and ask them what you can do for them, but good employees like me get nothing. I can tell you, if this keeps up you won't have a single good employee in this place.

What do you think the overall purpose of the final segment of this conversation was? _____

As the above exercise illustrates, the purposes in conversation change. Consequently, our response to the speaker should change to correspond to the changing motive of the speaker. That's part of the Language of Effective Listening.

Chapter Six

Troubleshooting

We are so resistant to anything that might disrupt our belief systems, our picture of the world, that we will unconsciously seek and allow ourselves to be drawn only to those views that we agree with.

—J. A. C. Brown

Every breakdown in communication brings some degree of loss in time, relationships, and effort. To get a handle on these breakdowns, a special formula has now been developed.[1] This formula or model was presented by Dr. Lyman Steil in *Effective Listening* and his other listening books. It is an excellent diagnostic tool for interpreting past situations, an application tool for use in the present, and a planning tool for preparing for future communication

It represents a far better approach than the all-too-common phenomenon of merely trying to get a word in edgewise without waiting for the speaker to finish.

Using the acronym *Success In Everyday Relationships* makes Dr. Steil's elegant model easy to remember. For emphasis, however, I prefer to separate two elements that he perceives to be inherent in his model. These additional elements are *Prepare* and *Synchronize*.[2]

PREPARE

The foundation for all success is 80 percent preparation and 20 percent application. By preparing, you do whatever is

ILLUSTRATION 6–1A
SIER Model: Identify and Repair Breakdowns in Communication

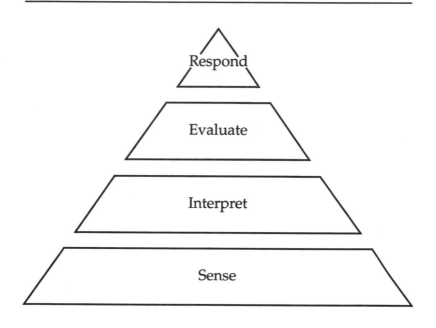

necessary to be able to listen. Like any good investment, preparing to listen pays big dividends. The payoff may not come immediately but will develop over time. By developing the habit of preparing, you gradually build up your investment. President Abraham Lincoln said, "I spend one third of my preparation in preparing for what I will say to the other person. I spend two thirds of my preparation in anticipating what the other person will say to me."[3] Here is an example of a breakdown in listening on the Prepare level.

George and Joanne are working together on a new process. A memo was sent to them saying that a third person having experience with similar projects was joining their team. This person had several innovative ideas, and the memo went on to share three of the most significant ones.

ILLUSTRATION 6–1B
PSSIER

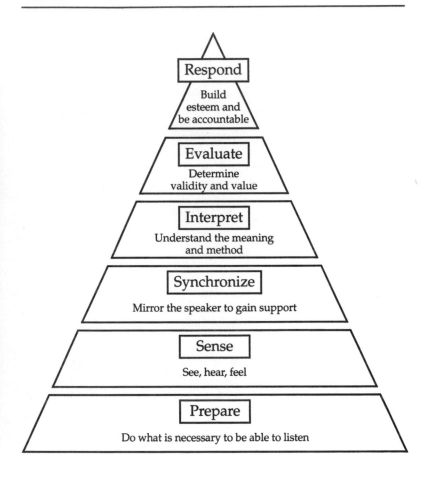

The following conversation took place a week after the memo was delivered.

George.

   Hi Joanne, I saw your door open and thought I'd take the opportunity to discuss the new process with you.

Joanne.

Come in, George. I have been anxious to get your reaction to several suggestions that Bill made.

George [Surprised].

What suggestions, Joanne? I didn't know Bill had anything to do with this project.

Five minutes of reading and thought preparation would have made George ready. Instead, he stole time from Joanne as she had to explain to him what Bill said.

Preparation Self-Check

How often are you prepared to listen? Review the following statements and put a check mark by the items that need future attention.

1. I try to get sufficient rest before important meetings.
2. I learn as much as possible about an individual or subject before the meeting.
3. I make a mental note or list of unfamiliar subjects or words that I hear from individuals with whom I have frequent conversations.
4. I carefully choose a place in a conference or other listening situation that will decrease distractions and increase my ability to listen.
5. I plan important conversations for the proper time and place.
6. I anticipate what emotionally laden subjects, people, or terms might come up in a conversation and then practice controlling myself.
7. I have calls held during important meetings.
8. I have pen and paper in hand when I answer the telephone.

SENSE

Hearing, seeing, feeling, and even, yes, smelling what the person said is sensing the communication. Many of the

breakdowns in communication occur at this level. The listener never heard, didn't see, or didn't feel what was being
communicated by the speaker. You have to be highly selective on this level, because you could never survive all the
sensory input of human communication, let alone the mean-
ingful noise of our environment. To protect ourselves from
the glut of sound, we learn to discriminate and respond to
selected frequencies and qualities of sound. We are also
environmentally, relationally, and culturally selective: we
automatically tune things out on each of these levels.

Sensing is also affected by interest, emotion, and bias. As
a result, we build habits that can militate against our hearing
many things that are or will be important to our lives. We
cannot listen to everything, but we can try to keep ourselves
flexible to strengthen our ability to hear against the harden-
ing of our mental arteries. Nationwide panic resulted on
October 30, 1938, from Orson Welles's broadcast "War of
the Worlds." Listeners believed aliens from Mars had in-
vaded New Jersey. Where did the communication breakdown occur? Some missed the announcement that this was
a fictitious drama. Others allowed fear to override their
initial understanding of the situation, especially when they
saw their terror-stricken neighbors.

A Breakdown of Listening at the Sense Level

The general manager and supervisor had a lengthy early
morning meeting. At the conclusion of the meeting, the
general manager said, "By the way, that meeting has been
changed to 2:30. It was 3:30. Did you get that?"

Supervisor.

Yeah, I got it.

However, the supervisor showed up at the meeting at 3:30.

General Manager.

Where were you; the meeting was at 2:30?

Supervisor.

You told me the meeting was at 3:30.

Clearly, the supervisor did not hear the words spoken by the general manager.

Sensing Self-Assessment

Do you sense everything necessary to get on the same wavelength with the speaker? Answer the following questions, and put a check mark by the items that need attention.

1. In conversation, I look at the speaker as much as possible without staring.
2. I am aware of changes in a person's rate, pitch, and loudness of speech.
3. I am aware of the feelings that the speaker is conveying or not conveying, that is, anger, fear, sadness, happiness, surprise, disgust, or neutrality.
4. When I am sad, angry, or excited, it is easy for me to pay attention to someone.
5. I am conscious of changes in a person's eye movements, facial expressions, posture, and gestures.
6. When I cannot avoid and/or remove environmental distractions, I concentrate more intently on the speaker.

SYNCHRONIZE

Synchronizing means gaining rapport with the speaker by adopting a similar body stance, vocal, and facial cues. Among essential communication skills, this one is least understood by the hundreds of managers and professionals who have completed our computerized listening inventory.

You cannot synchronize unless you have sensed what the person is conveying. Getting in sync is automatic if you sincerely concentrate on seeing, hearing and feeling what the speaker is saying. Personality conflicts most often arise from differences in communication style, resulting in a lack of synchronization. We are automatically in sync with those who are like us. We tend to appreciate and feel comfortable with those who communicate as we do, and are uncomfortable and discontent with those who do not. Without conscious effort, we often break the communication link at this level with those who communicate with a different style.

Communication Breakdown at the Synchronizing Level

Dave and Lydia have worked together in development for six months. The following conversation took place at the conclusion of a meeting about their joint project. The "report" mentioned was submitted by the marketing department as a summary of the application of their work.

Dave.

I didn't like the organization of the report.

Lydia.

Come on, Dave, you don't mean *that* bothered you?

Dave.

So long, Lydia, I have to be going.

Lydia.

Now you have to leave? What's the hurry?

Dave.

Bye, Lydia.

Communication without rapport is difficult and uncomfortable. If Lydia had sincerely reflected Dave's feelings in an understanding way before disagreeing with him, she would have established rapport and the conversation could have been constructive. Instead, Dave went away angry, and Lydia was confused.

Synchronize Self-Assessment

How often do you suffer a breakdown in communication at the synchronization level? These breakdowns are often called *personality conflicts*. They are a mismatch in communication style. Review the following items and ask yourself how often you have tried these techniques with a personality mismatch.

1. I share experiences when I have felt the same emotion that the speaker is feeling.
2. I communicate an understanding of the thoughts and feelings of others before stating a contrary position.
3. I do not change the subject until either the speaker is finished or the speaker has agreed to let me change the subject.
4. When I become aware that we don't have rapport, I try to match my gestures to the style and intensity of the speaker.
5. While communicating with different personality types, I match my facial expression with that of the speaker.
6. When seeking rapport, I match my rate of speech, tone of voice, pitch, and modulation to that of the speaker.

INTERPRET

I know you believe you understand what you think I said, but I am not sure you realize that what you heard is not what I meant.

—Anonymous

Sense and synchronization both affect interpretation. If the message is not sensed and synchronized, it cannot be accurately interpreted. To interpret is to understand the speaker's meaning by what the speaker is saying. To interpret accurately does not mean that we agree with the speaker. The problem is that many people interpret what is being said without adequate preparation. They haven't sensed what is being said nor synchronized with the speaker. Without proper preparation, our prejudices, backgrounds, presuppositions, and experiences produce a reflex causing us to anticipate what we think is going to be said. Untrained listeners are usually less than half right about what they anticipate is going to be said.

That we understand as much as we do is phenomenal. We do not understand how understanding happens. This ability is deeply buried in the matrix of the human brain, the terra incognita of the universe. How any child learns to speak and understand simply by listening to the voices of his language community is a miracle that no amount of study and thought have explained. How anyone, child or adult, can understand any language in all its complexity and amazing variety is equally inexplicable and even more mysterious. Just to utter all the possible English sentences of 20 words would require 10 trillion years. All of us utter sentences from time to time that were never before heard on earth.

To see the distinction between interpreting and sensing or synchronizing, carefully think about this statement: "A caterpillar is eating everything in sight!" Answer the following questions about your understanding of the caterpillar and what it is doing. Remember words comprise only 7 percent of the message.

1. When you think of the caterpillar, is it a big one or a small one? How much would you estimate that it weighs?

2. How much noise is it making while it is "eating"?

3. Describe the sound.

Thousands of people in our workshops have pictured a caterpillar weighing an ounce or so, chewing leaves, making little or no sound at all. But the caterpillar I had in mind weighs thousands of pounds and is made by a manufacturer of heavy equipment. Its engine is roaring while it digs a large hole. We all see or hear the same message, but we interpret it differently. I believe that most breakdowns in communication take place before or at this level in the model.

When you identify where a breakdown in communication takes place, you can work on solving the problem. In looking at the PSSIER model, always go to the base of the triangle and work your way up. The first question to ask is, "Was the listener prepared to listen?" If we can answer yes to this question, move on to the next level. "Did the listener see, hear, and feel what the speaker said?" Answering yes to this question enables you to go on. "Did the listener get in sync with the speaker?" If the answer is no at this or any of the lower levels, a domino effect follows, with breakdowns coming at the higher levels. At the interpretation level, ask if the listener understood what was seen, heard, and felt. By asking these questions, you will learn to discern the difference between being prepared to listen, sensing a message, synchronizing with the messenger, and understanding what that message means. Each step in the model is prerequisite to the next. You also learn to interpret the purpose behind the message.

Communication Breakdowns at the Interpretation Level

The following conversation took place in a major automaker's plant. It came at the end of a discussion about things to do for the next day.[4]

Maria.

Listen, Harry, how about having your people finish these cost studies for me?

Harry.

I can handle that.

[Next day.]

Maria.

Harry, did you finish those cost studies?

Harry.

No.

Maria.

Why not? You said you would.

Harry.

I did not.

Maria.

What are you talking about? You told me yesterday that you would finish them.

Harry.

What are you talking about? I never said anything of the kind.

Maria heard what Harry said, but she thought, "I can handle that" meant that Harry would do it by the next day. Harry meant that he was capable of doing it, but not that he would do it. Both parties were sincere. Both were wrong about what the other intended to convey.

The next breakdown is a misunderstanding between two co-workers. The third party, Bob, the manager, is trying to bring healing to a fractured relationship between Jim and Vicky.[5]

Bob [On phone].

Listen, Jim. I think the best way to clear up this problem is for you and Vicky to get together.

Jim.

I agree.

Bob.

O.K. then. I'll talk to you later and ask you how it turned out. [Two days later.]

Bob [As a woman walks into his office].

Hello, Vicky.

Vicky.

Hi! Hey, you know, Jim never called me.

Bob.

Really!

[Picking up the phone.]

I'll call him.

[Dialing.]

Hello, Jim. This is Bob. I have Vicky here in my office, and she tells me you haven't called her yet.

Jim.

I wasn't supposed to call her. She was supposed to call me. She started this whole thing. Why would I call her to set up a meeting?

In this breakdown, Jim heard the actual words used by Bob, but he interpreted them differently than Vicky did.

Interpretation Self-Assessment

Do you accurately understand what the speaker means by what that person is intending to convey? Answer the following questions, and put a check mark by the items that need attention.

1. I ask speakers to clarify what I do not understand.
2. I restate or paraphrase what a speaker has said to make certain that I have understood the individual.
3. I can tell when someone is trying to persuade me.
4. I ask questions to encourage individuals to express their opinions.
5. I listen for a speaker's major ideas and do not get lost in the details.
6. I pay more attention to a speaker's content than to appearance and manner of delivery.

EVALUATE

Nobody can judge a case unless he listens to all the arguments on both sides.

—Thomas Aquinas

If you conclude that the message was sensed, the messenger and you are in sync, and the message understood, proceed to the evaluation level. Evaluation is the sentinel at the gate that "puts a value" on what we hear and understand.

Evaluation is affected by unconscious assumptions, as happens, for example, when you reject a communication because of the way the speaker is dressed.

Evaluation is also affected by beliefs and expectations. We tend to respond to others with our evaluation before we have understood the message. Carl Rogers, Eli Porter, Sr., and associates tested helping professionals to find out which kind of response was given first: evaluation, interpretation, support, probing, or understanding. "They are most commonly given, they discovered, in that order. Evaluation . . . came first."[6] But part of being a good listener is to sort out objectively what you hear and to be able to come to reliable conclusions.

The danger lies in disagreeing before you fully understand. To understand does not mean that you agree, so when you disagree, try to disagree agreeably.

Follow these basic principles at the evaluation level. First, does the information seem to have any value for you? Is it relevant? This may be difficult to determine, because you don't know what the future holds.

Second, does the information have validity? Is it accurate?

Generally, we are hooked into listening because we accept the validity of the message. One theory contends that "in order to understand what another person is saying, you must assume it is true and try to imagine what it could be true of."[7] But once you decide that the message is probably valid, you must decide if it has any value for you. That is sometimes a more difficult question to answer than the validity question. An extended period may pass before you can profitably use the information. To determine the value of the message, it may be necessary to delay a final evaluation for a more deliberate analysis, particularly when the information is very long, complicated, or critical.

An evaluation pushes the other person away. Whether it is approving or disapproving, evaluation is judgmental.

Close-up videotapes of people in conversation show that the face gives an unconscious shock signal when an evaluation is received. A vertical wrinkle appears between the eyes for a split second as the eyebrows pull together in the universal sign of anxiety or pain. No matter how subtle the judgment, it makes an impact, and the impact is the same whether you judge the person or the message.[8] Knowing that evaluations given at the wrong time can prevent effective listening, learn the art of giving nonverbal responses that communicate understanding. Wait patiently for the proper time to vocalize your evaluative responses. Frequently, when the right time comes, the evaluation that seemed important earlier is no longer needed.

Communication Breakdowns at the Evaluation Level

George.

Bill, please finish up the accounting procedure report.

Bill.

O.K., George.

At the end of the day, George asks, "Will you bring the accounting procedure report to my office, Bill?"

Bill didn't give the information enough importance. He was tired and had been struggling with a problem employee and gave the order a low priority. The result of his improper evaluation? He got chewed out.

* * * * * *

Barbara.

Wayne, please get me the final figures ASAP.

Wayne.

You bet, Barbara, I'll have them for you before lunch.

But Wayne spent too much time on the report and let his day-to-day responsibilities go. He gave Barbara's request too much importance because he thought she wanted him to.

Evaluation Self-Assessment

Do you properly evaluate the information being sent? Answer the following questions, and put a check mark by the items that need future attention.

1. I weigh factual evidence carefully before I make a decision.

2. It is easy for me to pay attention to someone I don't like, as long as the person knows what he or she is talking about.

3. It is easy for me to disagree with someone I like very much.

4. Even though someone uses words that I find personally offensive, I am attentive to what the speaker is saying.

5. When I am receiving criticism, I discern and admit to any element that is true.

6. I listen for a speaker's major ideas and do not get lost in the details.

7. I pay more attention to a speaker's content than to appearance and manner of delivery.

8. I find something of value in what every speaker has to say.

9. I differentiate facts from opinions.

RESPOND

The technique which I was obliged to develop in those unimportant early posts has served me in later years for my imperial audiences: to give oneself totally to each person throughout the brief duration of a hearing; to reduce the world for a moment to this banker, that veteran or that widow; to accord to these individuals, each so different though each confined naturally within the narrow limits of a type, all the polite attention which at the best moments one gives to oneself.

—Roman Emperor Hadrian

Response is the apex of the PSSIER model and is the ultimate measure of how well we listen. An effective listener answers a speaker's communication in a way that communicates understanding of what was said and felt, then accepts responsibility for that understanding. In your response, you feed back to the speaker your understanding of the other person's problems and needs and take responsibility to follow through. If a breakdown occurs at the response level, ask, "Did the listener do what the listener decided to do? Did the listener forget to do it? Did the listener not have enough time, information, or ability to do it? Has the person done a poor job because of a lack of time, information, or ability.

If you have the skill to fulfill all of the other prerequisites well but do not respond appropriately, you create a breakdown in communication. Avoid reactions that shoot from the hip. Responses should be thoughtfully based on proper preparation, sensing, synchronizing, interpretation, and evaluation.

The ultimate listening goal is to make the right evaluations and responses. The wrong responses and nonresponses can destroy not only communication but also relationships. Response completes the cycle of communication by indicating in the right way that you have understood.

* * * * *

Try to identify where the breakdown in communication occurred in the following stories.

A bar owner locked up his place at 2 A.M. and went home to sleep. He had been in bed only a few minutes when the phone rang. "What time do you open up in the morning?" he heard an obviously inebriated man inquire.

The owner was so furious, he slammed down the receiver and went to back to bed. A few minutes later there was another call, and he heard the same voice ask the same question. "Listen," the owner shouted, "there's no sense in asking me what time I open because I wouldn't let a person in your condition in . . ."

"I don't want to get in," the caller interjected. "I want to get out."[9]

* * * * *

WHERE IS THE BREAKDOWN IN COMMUNICATION?

As a responder, it is easy to get on someone's case and assume that person evaluated the communication differently from you and is going against your will. But that person may have never understood what you said, or may not have heard, felt, and seen what you said in the first place.

Similar strengths and weakness were found in individuals who were expected to rise higher in their organization than they did and those who made it to the top. The difference most often cited between the two groups is that the derailed group is more insensitive to others. That is not the only reason for derailment. Some commit the "unforgivable sin," betraying a trust. "Betrayal" rarely has anything to do with honesty that is a given. Rather, it involves one-upmanship or failure to follow through on promises. This betrayal wreaks havoc on trust. Your responses tell who you are and what you think of others. They help people to decide how much they can trust you and place confidence in you.

Response Self-Assessment

1. I do not try to change the subject until either the speaker is finished or speaker has agreed to let me change the subject.

2. When I am receiving criticism, I discern and admit to any element that is true.

3. I wait without interrupting until the speaker is through. Then I pause, think, and respond.

4. I find something of value in what every speaker has to say.

5. In a conversation, I listen more than I speak.

6. I keep privately shared information confidential.

7. I try to raise the self-esteem of everyone I listen to.

8. I consistently follow through on what is expected of me after a conversation.

PSSIER SAW-TOOTHED MODEL

This model expands the static, "frozen frame moment" to show how our interactions progress through time. It simply captures that we switch back and forth between sender and receiver roles. We prepare, sense, synchronize, interpret, evaluate, and respond simultaneously. Communication becomes even more complex when you add other people to the conversation.

ILLUSTRATION 6–2
Triangle—PSSIER Saw-Toothed Model

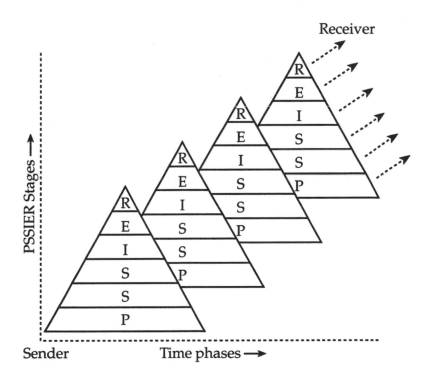

Chapter Seven

RELATIONS and Roadblocks

Everyone should be quick to listen and slow to speak.

—St. James

Previously mentioned models help you to identify where breakdowns have already occurred, the RELATIONS model prevents these breakdowns from happening.

The RELATIONS model is a surefire way to develop effective listening skills and positive relations. First, we discuss the model, and then we review the roadblocks that often hinder its use.

Jerry had an urgent need when she walked into her supervisor's office. "George, do you have a minute?" George barely looked up from his desk. "You again! Get to the point, Jerry, I'm in a hurry."

Jerry quit her job that day. Trying to communicate with George had become too stressful and unproductive. After 15 years of service in the company, Jerry still liked her work, but the abrasive manner of her supervisor was too much to take. Her many attempts to build a relationship with her supervisor always led to a dead end. In spite of the difficult relationship, she always gave her best. Now she was getting an ulcer. Trying to work with her super was more difficult than it was worth.

Jerry is not alone in her reaction to this job-related stress. Thousands of workers quit their jobs every day for similar reasons. Broken relationships are a primary cause of stress and the number one reason employees leave their companies. Seventy-five percent of workers in the United States admit that they do not work up to their capacity.[1] Building better relationships through effective listening will increase worker satisfaction and productivity.

THE *RELATIONS* MODEL

Most people go through life without a good model of how to be an effective listener. The RELATIONS model for effective listening provides you with a basic, effective map to get around the Dirty Dozen Roadblocks. The acronym *RELATIONS* was coined by my associate, Dr. Ken Boa, and me. It includes the basic elements of an effective listening model and encapsulates the essence of what the Language of Effective Listening is about. Effective listening builds trusting relationships. From trusting relationships comes greater productivity.

Practice the RELATIONS model with the Favored Five, the people you are aiming to relate to more meaningfully, and with those who have been offended by your responses to their problems.

R Is for Relaxed Tension

A nonjudgmental, positive attitude helps the listener be aware of communication purposes. When you are tense, it is more difficult to concentrate on what the speaker is saying. Tension causes you to think more about yourself and your response than about the speaker.

E Is for Eye Contact without Staring

The way the person moves his eyes and the way the eyes dilate or don't dilate is an unconscious, nonverbal communication to you about what the person is thinking and feeling. If the person's eyes dilate it's probably because the person's emotions have been triggered. The emotion may be anger, fear, or joy. You may not be certain which emotion was touched, but you may be certain that an emotion was affected.

Look directly at the speaker and appear to be attentive. If you have trouble looking at the speaker's eyes, look at the forehead. From several feet away, the speaker usually cannot tell the difference. By observing the speaker's eyes you will be looking at the "light of his or her soul." The eyes will tell you much about what the speaker means by what the speaker is saying.

L Is for Lean in toward the Speaker

This body stance communicates an openness to the speaker and encourages that individual to say more. *Proxemics*, the study of space and human relations to space, is very revealing. In some cultures, people like to be very close to one another when they talk. In Greece, Brazil, and Japan, proximity of less than three feet from the speaker is normal. To back away from the speaker can be regarded as an insult. In Germany and some Scandinavian countries, three feet would, in many business situations, be too close. Sensitivity to distance requires individual adjustment to find the best distance that is most comfortable for the other person.

A Is for Active Silence

Without your saying anything verbally, this skill communicates to the speaker that you are listening, thinking, and trying to understand what the speaker is saying. Usually, a

ILLUSTRATION 7–1
Effective Listeners Lean Toward Speaker

R	E	L	A	T	I	O	N	S
Relaxed Tension	Eye Contact	Lean Toward the Speaker	Active Silence	Tell Me More	Involved Feedback	Open Posture	Noise Control	Squared Off

silence of two or three seconds is sufficient to decide if the speaker is finished and wants you to respond verbally. Often in the conversation, after this flicker of silence, the good stuff comes out. The person ends a thought and sees that you're really listening. Then the person may go on with what they *really* wanted to say. Remain attentive. Think about what the speaker is saying. Put on your *EARS:* silently Evaluate, Anticipate, Review, and Summarize.

T Is for Tell Me More

Use nonverbal feedback to encourage the speaker to go on. When you match the intensity and manner of the speaker with facial expressions, gestures, nods, and responses like "uh-huh, Oh, mm-hmm," you encourage the individual to continue.

I Is for Involved Feedback

Use verbal responses to involve yourself with the thought process and feelings of the speaker. Play back some of the same words that are used. Paraphrase the speaker's thoughts. Ask appropriate questions for clarification. Ask yourself, "How would I feel if I were the speaker?" Then take a chance and tell the speaker how you think that individual feels. Be willing to be corrected if you are inaccurate.

O Is for Open Posture

Your arms may be crossed tightly across your chest because you're cold or tired. But subliminally this stance may create in the mind of the other person the impression that you're closed to what the individual is saying. This body language is very important. You emanate more than 700,000 nonverbal cues during the course of 4,000 intelligible messages during any typical day. As the nonverbal communications are being given out, a person subliminally responds. Uncross your arms to show that you are receptive. Subconsciously, this movement helps the speaker believe that you are open to thoughts and feelings, and enables the speaker to be more open with you.

N Is for Noise Control

You need to prevent both internal and external noises from distorting the message or from deafening you to the speaker's message. Some internal noises are caused by physiological problems, like a headache or tiredness. Psychological noises are created by a recent argument or by emotionally charged words or subject matter, whether positive or negative. External noises can be other people talking, a telephone ringing, a television set, or an air conditioner going off or on. Try to recognize the noise momentarily and then either get rid of it or concentrate through it.

S Is for Square Off

"Square off," or directly face the speaker. Not only does this position demonstrate interest, but also it enables you to see and hear much better than if you were not facing the speaker. Obviously, there are occasions when it is not possible to square off, for example, when you are walking side by side. With a desk between you and a person in your office you are squared off if you are sitting directly opposite, but the desk is a barrier. If possible, set a chair alongside your desk, so you don't have the barrier of the desk separating you and the person.

HOW TO OVERCOME THE DIRTY DOZEN ROADBLOCKS

Dr. Rich Walters identified what he calls the "Dirty Dozen Roadblocks To Effective Listening."[2] These are things we commonly do that often turn out to be counterproductive to building better communication and more positive relationships. Examine this list reflectively, identify the responses you overuse, then remove the roadblocks.

Good listeners help people to solve their problems. They resist setting up conversational roadblocks. Instead, they make their responses "road signs" that help the individuals see and hear their own thoughts and feelings.

You will accomplish more and build better relationships by allowing others to come to their own conclusions. At times, these Dirty Dozen Roadblocks can actually be stepping stones to effective communication, positive relationships, and greater productivity. Like fine spices, properly used they can benefit a conversation. Just remember too much salt spoils the pie and gives you high blood pressure, too! Seventy-five percent of the time people are better off solving their own problems, 99 percent of the time they will be far more responsive to our suggestions when we show an understanding of what they think and feel.

"Before responding, ask yourself five questions to help put yourself in the other's place. If I were the speaker: (a) Would I be thinking positively or negatively about myself as a person? (b) What would I be feeling? (c) What would I be wishing? (d) What would I be thinking about doing? (e) What conflicts would I be experiencing?"[3]

Two yellow lights flash at this juncture. If you consistently respond empathetically, you may become the other's counselor. To avoid that kind of relationship use more "seasoning" in your responses. If you respond mechanically instead of naturally, you will undo the trust you are trying to build.

FIND THE ROADBLOCKS TO YOUR COMMUNICATION SUCCESS

Examine the 12 roadblocks listed below. Then follow this procedure:

1. Place a check mark by those (roadblock) responses that most often characterize you.
2. Write the initials of the person or persons you offend with these responses.
3. Write the kind of response that you will try to use from now on.

Notice that Roadblocks 1 through 5 are situations in which you refuse to recognize that the person has the capability to handle problems.

Roadblock 1. Giving direction, commanding. The drill sergeant in you tells the other person to do something, gives orders, or commands instead of reflecting back to that person an understanding of the problem.

Statement: "Adding a new shift to the floor is going to double our administrative responsibilities."

Roadblock: "You should appreciate the increased productivity instead of complaining."

Initials: _____

Suggested Response: "You are glad that the company is doing well, but you are concerned that you are getting more than your share of the added work."

Your Response: _____

Roadblock 2. Advising, suggesting, or offering solutions, or telling the other person how to solve problems. In setting up this roadblock, you play the role of the parent and communicate condescension to the speaker.

Statement: "My boss doesn't like it when any of his people leave even two minutes early."

Roadblock: "If for any reason you must leave early, check with your boss early in the day and request his permission. Promise to make up the time."

Initials: _____

Suggested response: "You are concerned about your boss's attitude toward those who leave early."

Your Response: _____

Roadblock 3. Warning, admonishing, threatening. Through these, you tell the other person what negative consequences will occur if that person does something. Like a hangman, you allude to the use of your power.

Statement: "What is the meaning of that memo we got in the mail this morning? I have a right to know and I'm going to start asking questions."

Roadblock: "Curiosity killed the cat. You start asking a bunch of questions and you'll get yourself in trouble."

Initials: _____

Suggested Response: "You feel that the memo was too vague and raised some questions that you have a right to have answered."

Your Response: _____

_____

Roadblock 4. Moralizing, preaching. In this response, we assume the superior role of the prophet with divine insight.
Statement: "Adding a new shift to the floor is going to double our administrative responsibilities. That isn't fair."
Roadblock: "You should appreciate the added responsibility instead of complaining."

Initials: _____

Suggested Response: "You feel the added responsibility isn't right."

Your Response: _____

_____

Roadblock 5. Persuading, arguing, lecturing. Using "facts," counter arguments, logic, and information like a salesman to influence the speaker with your own opinions instead of empathizing with the speaker.
Statement: "I have two candidates for that new secretarial position. I'm going to choose youth over experience. You can't teach an old dog new tricks."
Roadblock: "If you had more information you wouldn't make that mistake. First, your younger candidate has not yet shown the ability to fit into the culture. You don't even know if the individual is capable of doing the work. Second, your

older candidate has proven ability and adaptability. This person has changed and grown with each new assignment over the past 10 years."

Initials: _____

Suggested Response: "Of the two candidates, you believe the youngest has the best chance of adapting to the new position."

Your Response: _____

Roadblocks 6 through 10 are personal put-downs, real ego crushers. In these responses, the speaker is given even less respect than with the first five responses. The individual is misunderstood and leaves the conversation much worse off than if that person never tried to share the problem.

Roadblock 6. Judging, criticizing, disagreeing, blaming. In this response, the speaker is being personally rejected. Negative judgments of the person's character rather than the individual's analysis of the problem being shared are this roadblock to communication.

Statement: "My performance appraisal was a shock."

Roadblock: "A real professional knows what the manager thinks of the work. You just haven't been paying attention."

Initials: _____

Suggested Response: "You feel you were taken by surprise."

Your Response: _____

Roadblock 7. Inappropriate praise. In this response, you flatter the speaker or offer a positive evaluation or judgment without listening, thereby short circuiting the communication.

You imply that what the speaker is saying is so embarrassing that the individual shouldn't be heard.

Statement: "My spouse and I are having a tough time. We don't have much to say to each other anymore."

Roadblock: "I heard about the report that you turned in last week. Great job."

Initials: _____

Suggested Response: "It sounds like things are tough at home."

Your Response: _____

_____

Roadblock 8. Name-calling, ridiculing, shaming. This response makes the speaker feel foolish, often stereotyping or categorizing him. This is the mugger in action, catching our prey unaware.

Statement: "Look at the awful way that person dresses. You'd think that person would know better."

Roadblock: "You people that criticize are all alike. Look at yourselves sometimes. You're all guilty of the problem you see in others."

Initials: _____

Suggested Response: "You would like to see that person get some instruction in proper dress."

Your Response: _____

_____

Responses 9 through 12 implicitly deny that a problem even exists. We assume "it's just in the person's imagination."

Roadblock 9. Focusing on the person, not the problem. In this response, we play the part of a psychiatrist, telling a person what his motives are or analyzing why he is doing or saying something.

Statement: "When is this fatigue going to stop! It seems like I have been tired ever since vacation."

Roadblock: "I think you're really saying that you don't like your work."

Initials: _____

Suggested Response: "You must really miss your old energy level. It's tough not knowing when you will feel like yourself again."

Your Response: _____

Roadblock 10. Withdrawing, distracting, humoring. This response is an attempt to distract the individual from the problem instead of helping the individual to explain it. Misused "humor" is like vinegar on an open wound.

Statement: "It cost more to repair my car than it is worth."

Roadblock: "Funny, isn't it, that beauty's only skin deep, but ugly's to the bone. Beauty fades away, but ugly holds its own. Ha, ha!"

Initials: _____

Suggested Response: "You feel like you have been taken for a ride on that repair bill."

Your Response: _____

Roadblock 11. Probing, questioning, interrogating, putting the person on defense or incorrectly assuming the problem. In this response, you act like the detective or prosecuting attorney trying to find motives or causes, searching for more information to help solve the problem.

Statement: "My assistant was late to work three times last week."

Roadblock: "Did you say you can be replaced?"

Initials: _____

Suggested Response: "Three times in one week, that's frustrating."

Your Response: _____

_____

Roadblock 12. Patronizing, condescending. Trying to make the other person feel better, talking the person out of the feelings, trying to make the feelings go away, denying the strength of the feelings, performing like a magician.

Statement: "I'm so angry I could chew nails. Everybody but me gets recognition for their work."

Roadblock: "That's too bad, a person like you being treated that way. But cheer up, we all have to go through that at some time."

Initials: _____

Suggested Response: "You recognize the value of your work. It would be nice for others to see it, too." (Or, "You respect your work, and it would be helpful for others to also respect the work you do.")

Your Response: _____

_____

You can build better relationships by making the RELATIONS model your own experience, or you can continue to set up roadblocks to mutual understanding. The skills outlined above work. Practice the RELATIONS model with a friend, and then move on to riskier relationships and enjoy the benefits of principles proven true by thousands of your successful associates.

Chapter Eight

The Control of Emotions

Each of us is an impregnable fortress that can be laid waste only from within.

—Timothy J. Flynn

Emotion brings color, meaning, fulfillment, and purpose to our lives. Through our emotions we taste the worst or the best of life. Emotions pull us down and lift us up. Emotional expression can turn monotonous, humdrum tasks into experiences beautiful and rich. Without emotion, life would be devoid of pain but also devoid of zest.

Hundreds of millions of dollars are spent each year to find out what touches your emotions. That information is used by merchandisers to push your emotional button, hoping to induce you to take particular action. The world of market research is rife with individuals and organizations well trained, highly skilled and motivated, and well paid to discover the emotional triggers of others.

Sometimes people unconsciously touch your emotions. Think about your home life. Who touches your emotions at home? Do these people know they touch your emotions? Are these individuals conscious of the words or actions that touch you? How do you respond when your emotions are affected? Think about your professional life. On most business teams you find different personalities with different ways of expressing feelings. Do the differences help or hinder you on the job?

We should be very grateful for emotion. Nevertheless, we must realize that when emotions go up, rationality goes down. Anyone who knows more about your emotional triggers than you do is in a position to control you. To have the control of your own emotions will free you to be all that you can possibly be.

EMOTIONS CAN BRING GAIN OR PAIN

The legendary football coach Vince Lombardi shared with corporation leader Lee Iacocca the importance of emotions to the success of a team. When talent, discipline, and coaching are about equal, emotion makes the difference. "If you are going to play together as a team, you've got to care for one another. You've got to *love* each other. The difference between mediocrity and greatness is the feeling these guys have for each other. . . . It's the same thing whether you are running a ball club or a corporation."[1]

* * * * *

He was working under the car when the bumper slid off the jack and pinned him under 1,500 pounds. He was doomed had his 112-pound mother not reached down and lifted the car off him. (Ripley's *Believe it or Not!*)

* * * * *

Every business and every person faces 1,500-pound problems with 112-pound bodies to handle crises. Without emotion it can't be done. Emotions bring gain. They can also bring blinding pain.

* * * * *

Once riding in old Baltimore
Heart filled, head-filled with glee, I saw a Baltimorean—keep
    looking straight at me
Now I was eight and very small
and he was no whit bigger,
And so I smiled, but he poked out his tongue
and called me "Nigger."
I saw the whole of Baltimore from May until December;
of all the things that happened there
that's all that I remember.
Countee Cullen

* * * * *

The negative side of emotions is witnessed in despair. Neurobiological research illustrates how necessary hope is to the survival drive. David Ingvar's research with Position Emission Tomography, (PET Scan) shows computer-generated pictures of the neocortex during different states of mind. Ingvar finds that the brain waves slow measurably when people cannot anticipate a positive future. A sense of hope is a big help in solving problems.[2]

Positive feelings mean a lot. They are not, however, the cure-all for every situation. In the 1930s, an Oklahoma high school football team was in an awful slump. They could not seem to win a game. Disappointed by the repeated defeats, a local oil man promised a brand new Ford for every player and coach if they won their next game. The team could hardly think of anything but victory. The coaches gave a pregame pep talk, and, as usual, the kids didn't pay attention. With a whoop and a holler they ran out onto the field to meet their opposition—and lost 38–0. Positive feelings help, but they must be combined with certain essentials.

SELF-CONTROL IN LISTENING

In the effective listener, indeed the effective person, emotions must always be subject to the faculties of reason and will. Difficulties and stress occur in the life of every human being on earth. Like the weather, circumstances change, and with change in circumstances comes a change in feelings. You never know what the next day or night might hold for you. Without the checks and balances of reason and will you could be on a perpetual emotional roller coaster.

We are almost always engaged in a subconscious monologue with ourselves. Nearly three-quarters of this self-talk is unfortunately negative. The subconscious mind believes whatever we tell it and will make the external reality conform to the internal image. Biochemical changes occur in the body in response to emotional input in the mind. These biochemical changes precipitate intense feelings that are impossible to ignore. In this way, our inner speech influences behavior, feelings, self-esteem, and, ultimately, how we listen. It's easier to act yourself into a better way of feeling than to feel your way into a better way of acting.

Bernice works in a tough business with a great deal of stress, compounded by a personality conflict with one of her colleagues. This associate seemed to take pleasure in making her life difficult. She tensed up and became defensive in this person's presence. Listening became especially difficult.

After identifying the need for emotional control, in private, Bernice practiced relaxation techniques and visualization of control. She was able to transfer her visualization in private to performance in public in a way that saved her job.

An effective listener knows how to control emotions in at least three areas: (1) with speakers, no matter who they are; (2) with subject matter, whatever it is; and (3) with language or words that are used, regardless of what they are.[3]

The speaker.   If you are positive toward an individual, you tend not to listen effectively. Without evaluating the message, you buy everything the speaker says because of your positive attitude toward that person. When you have negative regard for the speaker, response is equally nonobjective on the downside of the scale. The tendency is to turn the speaker off before that individual is finished making a case.

This predetermined judgment suggests that certain people have nothing worthwhile to say. Isn't it possible that even though you might not like a person, that individual may have insight or help that will be very important to you? I don't know the person who discovered penicillin. I might not even like that person, but I have benefited from what that individual did. To realize that people don't have to think or be like me to be effective and profitable is liberating. The kiss of death for the professional is not being able to get along with others! Can we afford *not* to control our emotions?

Emotional control is not neutrality, however. Neutrality is not necessarily a blessing. If you're neutral and not emotionally involved enough to care about a person or issue, you tend to go to sleep. Identify your emotions toward the significant people in your life. You may even want to keep a little notebook and log the initials of the people who come into your life during the course of the next 30 days. Put a plus, a minus, or a zero by the person's name. (Just be careful to keep your record where no one else will happen upon it! They might not yet have learned the value of emotional control!)

The subject matter.   What issues or subjects touch your emotions? Do you feel positive, neutral, or negative about them? Gun control. Women in combat. Computerized dating. Equal Rights Amendment. Capital punishment. Socialized medicine. Organized religion. Taxes. Pro-choice / right to life. Inflation. Foreign ownership of United States property.

What personal interest or experience predisposes you to positive or negative feelings on certain issues? Is retirement an emotional issue for you? Is job security an emotional issue? Promotion? Performance appraisal? What are the emotional issues in your life? Do you know what they are, and can you control your emotions when you hear people discussing these issues?

In college debates, students are taught to make a cogent presentation of an issue regardless of their personal prejudices and biases. Debaters have to be prepared to debate the pro or the con of a given issue. Just minutes before the debate starts, they are told which side they are going to argue. Whether presenting for or against the issue, success depends on having accurate information, interpreting it correctly, and responding appropriately, regardless of the debater's personal feelings about the issue. Adopting the exercise of looking at all sides of an issue in the privacy of your own mind would be a helpful way for you to practice emotional control.

The language. Certain terms elicit feelings of warmth, feelings of anger, feelings of fear. What terms touch your emotions? What words do you respond to positively and negatively?

What terms touch your emotions in a negative way? How do you respond to the following words? *Republican. Jock. Sex. Intellectual. Democrat. Liberal. Conservative. Pig. Honkie. Bastard. Strike. Discrimination. Kike. Bitch. Management. Labor.*

Among the measures you can take to end slavery to emotions are these: (1) Identify those people and things that trigger negative feelings and practice dealing with them. (2) Try aerobic exercises, meditate, pray, and think positively. (3) Stimulate the brain's production of serotonin—which calms and relaxes—by eating about an ounce and a half of carbohydrates, such as popcorn.

Emotions can affect our listening capacity in funny ways. It's logical to assume, for example, that if you feel positively toward an individual, you will be more interested in what that person says. Not always true. Experts point out that if a speaker is someone you like, you might just buy everything that is said without bothering to listen. For different reasons, of course, we tend also to tune out those for whom we have a negative regard.

Work at not allowing negative feelings to keep you from appreciating a person's potential value. That alone will go a long way to making you a better listener.

Certain words and subjects can be a special problem for listeners, too. They can easily deceive us. Be wary.

Emotional Control under Fire: "Verbal Self-Defense"

Just in proportion as he is sentient and restless, just in proportion as he reacts and reciprocates and penetrates, is the critic a valuable instrument.

—Henry James

Never do you need emotional control more than when you are receiving criticism. All criticism is not negative, but all criticism is judgmental and can be manipulative. From its Latin root *criticus* comes the concept of a neutral, objective appraisal of ideas and actions. Criticism, properly used, is a tool to encourage and enhance personal growth and relationships. Properly used, it will motivate people, encourage self-improvement, and teach and communicate needs and desires. Improperly used or interpreted, it can mislead or devastate.

Perhaps you have heard statements similar to these: "Come on, Dale. You've been around here for five years.

You know better than *that.*" Or, "Are you kidding? That idea is as old as the ages. I thought you had something new."

How would you react to positive statements such as these? "Wow, Terry, you've only been here a few days, and you've already got the idea how to do it!" Or, "That's a great idea. I'm glad to hear something new."

Why is the response to negative criticism often anger, frustration, or depression, making it difficult to respond effectively and constructively? It's not uncommon for the one criticized to respond with verbal or physical abuse. Even positive criticism can come across in a negative way. Sometimes it feels like condescension or manipulation. You can't be sure it wasn't insincere flattery. Are you satisfied with the way you respond to a positive critic of your work?

Both positive and negative criticism can be handled in the same way, with filters. Oil filters, coffee filters, air filters—the world is full of filters to eliminate impurities and distortions. The same principle applies to words. Use the appropriate "filters" to evaluate and respond to the message. You wouldn't pour coffee grounds into a cup and add water. Why allow all the information thrown at you to enter without filters?

The communication style filter. Virginia Satir identified five distinct styles or patterns of language behavior that people use under stress and that are useful in learning how people give criticism. Dr. Suzette Haden Elgin has done a masterful job of interpreting Satir and conveys her concepts through her series of books on *The Gentle Art of Verbal Self Defense.* Understand and identify these styles and you have the first filter through which to screen both positive and negative criticism. The style filter will help you profit from constructive criticism and protect yourself from negative criticism.

The Placater. Placaters are fearful people, concerned that others will become angry and cut them off personal inter action. In the movie *Marty,* the lead character played by Ernest

ILLUSTRATION 8–1
Effective Listeners Control Their Emotions

Borgnine is with his buddy in a bar, trying to decide what to do that night.

Marty.

What do you want to do tonight?

Friend.

Oh, I don't know, what do you want to do?

Marty.

I don't care, what do you think?

The ineffective conversation goes on with each afraid of hurting the other and thereby losing the friendship.

When criticizing, Placaters have a hard time telling the flat, naked truth. They are more concerned with how the other person will feel about them than in getting the point across.

The Blamer.   Blamers feel powerless. They feel that no one cares about them. To compensate, the Blamer tries to take charge and show who is the boss. The Blamer's criticism tends to exaggerate statements to make sure that the point was made.

"You're always *overspending* your budget."

"You *never* do things right."

The Computer. The Computer is afraid to disclose feelings. A good example of a Computer was Mr. Spock on "Star Trek." Computers will block out all emotion from their voices or words when they give criticism.

"Without question, the job can be done in a different way."

"People can logically conclude that the solution lies in adopting the new policy."

The Distracter. The Distracter does not maintain any one of the personality types. Instead, the person shifts from Computer to Blamer to Placater. The individual feels the compulsion to say something and say it right now! But since the Distracter doesn't know what to say, an incoherent mix of thoughts follows.

"The bill could have been paid on time, don't you think? Well maybe not, but its always being paid late. Anyway, a rational person would be very concerned."

When a Distracter criticizes, you are hit with a diverse set of feelings simultaneously. To get to the element of truth, if there is one, takes a lot of sifting through the Distracter's criticism.

The Leveler. The person using this style tells it like it is. When the Leveler is sincere, that individual is using the most helpful of the communicating styles from which to accept criticism.

"Three times out of the last eight you requested documentary support for our stats. On each occasion you found our work accurate. We are not dealing with a critical matter here. Why not let it go *this* time? Your request will slow us up, and we won't meet our deadline."

That is not a verbal attack. It is a thoughtful request. Sometimes the Leveler is assumed to be the enemy, and the "nice guy" upstairs is looked upon as your supporter. The truth may be just the other way around.

The following examples show the five styles being used in a "crisis" situation. Five people are trapped in an elevator stuck between the sixth and seventh floors.[3]

Placater.

> Oh, I *hope* I didn't do anything to cause this. I surely didn't *mean* to.

Blamer.

> Which of you idiots was fooling around with the buttons?

Computer.

> There is undoubtedly some perfectly logical reason why this elevator isn't moving. Certainly there is no cause whatever for alarm.

Distracter.

> Did one of you hit the Stop button? Oh, I didn't *mean* that; of course, none of you would do anything like that. It is, however, extremely easy to do that sort of thing by accident. *Why* do things like this only happen to me?

Leveler.

> Personally, I'm scared.[4]

When you aren't sure which style you should use to respond to criticism, use the computer mode. Control your emotions and be as objective as possible. Then, as you gain equilibrium, synchronize with the speaker. Recognition of the differing style types gains you greater objectivity in evaluating the criticism and puts you in a better position to judge whether or not you need to seek more information. You're free to decide how best to respond.

Exercise

Think once again of the Favored Five, the people with whom you are going to build your relationship over the next 30 days. Try to identify the usual styles they use when giving you criticism. Placater, Blamer, Computer, Distracter, or Leveler.

Initials _____   Style _____
Initials _____   Style _____
Initials _____   Style _____
Initials _____   Style _____
Initials _____   Style _____

The truth filter. If the feedback being given has any validity, find that valid point. It may contain only one "kernel" amidst a bushel of chaff. Look for it. Then admit to the valid point, and sincerely thank the critic for the information.

This process establishes that you are a reasonable person. You enable the criticizer to focus on the point you agree on and to forget the overstatement. You protect your self-esteem and the esteem of the criticizer. You may gain valuable insight. The perspective of others will help you become all you can be! "Listen to advice and accept instruction and, in the end, you will be wise."

Critic: "You are *always* late."

Response: "Marty, I was late *today*, but that won't happen again."

The emotion filter. Separate the criticism from the criticizer! Emotional criticism may have roots in the criticizer's emotional needs. His own needs, hurts, or fears may cause him to charge into an attack before assessing the timing or appropriateness of the criticism. Using the emotion filter, you will consider the source and determine the appropriateness. As you run the speaker's words through the emotion filter, you shift the spotlight from you to them.

The persuasive techniques filter. Isolate any part of the message that uses persuasive techniques and resist them long enough to ask relevant questions. Your best defense is to follow the advice, "Know yourself!" Which of the following techniques would most likely influence you?

Bandwagon: "Everybody's doing it! Get on the bandwagon with us."

Card stacking: Using illustrations, facts, opinions carefully selected to make the best or worst possible case for an idea, product, or person. The speaker omits anything that may give you another point of view.

Glittering generality: "Virtue" words like *democracy, justice,* or *motherhood* are associated with idea or product being pushed.

Name-calling: Labels are used to bait the hearer into condemning something or someone without evidence. With no consideration of the ethics involved, a reputation can quickly and easily be destroyed.

Plain folks: This technique associates an idea or product with the common man who is "just like you."

Testimonial: A highly accepted individual or group is associated with an idea or product, hoping to influence its acceptance. Association with a disliked personality is made if the purpose is to influence rejection of the idea or product.

The perspective filter. Determine the false assumption. If you believe an invalid assumption is inherent in the criticism, identify and reject the false assumption.

Critic: "If you had been *early,* the project would have been approved."

Response: "I don't believe that the entire project rests upon the *time* of my arrival."

Balance the piece of criticism against all you have accomplished in your life. The scales have to weigh in your favor.

Critic: "Harry, you *really* missed the boat on this one."

Response: "Hey, *nobody* bats a thousand, not even the boss. We'll get 'em *next* time."

Fine, you say, but by the time I run the message through all these filters, my criticizer will be long gone."[5]

This situation can happen, especially when someone gives you a quick shot and leaves. What you can do when you are unable to give an immediate response to criticism is to decide the right filter, then mentally review a proper response. This mental exercise will prepare you for an encounter you can respond to verbally. With a little practice, you will be able to run messages through your filters almost instantaneously and be ready to respond.

Here are four immediate responses to negative criticism. Use them with discretion. Your voice "quality" will be most important. This quality includes pitch, nasality, volume, breathiness, harshness, and timbre. Albert Mehrabian and other highly respected researchers discovered that 38 percent of the meaning of what we say is found, not in the words themselves, but in how we say them. The work of Manfred Clynes as reported by Suzette Haden Elgin, demonstrates that "intonation that leaps sharply up and down in pitch, that cuts words off choppily, that punches at certain words and phrases, that clings to a straight, monotonous line . . ." are linear and angular rather than curved and communicate negative emotions. Positive emotions that are more likely to elicit a positive response are expressed by smooth, curving intonation.[6]

Quick Responses to Negative Criticism

❒ Short circuit the message.
❒ Communicate your feelings.
❒ Put yourself in their place.
❒ Ask for more information.

1. Short circuit the message.

Critic: [Manager bursts into your office.] "Where are those reports? Aren't you finished yet?"

Response: [Smiling.] "Good morning, Chris. How are you?"

Critic: "Huh? Oh, good morning."

2. Communicate your feelings.

Response: [Calmly.] "Chris, you're not helping me. You're making me nervous. Please leave me alone and I'll be finished."

3. Put yourself in their place.

Response: "Chris, I know this is important. You can help me by making sure that no one disturbs me and by seeing that the copy machine is free." (It gives a nervous manager something to do.)

4. Ask for more information. Frequently, there are a number of reasons why the person criticized your work. The initial point of criticism may be insufficient for you to profit from. If more information will help you, ask for it. This is the easiest and safest of the quick responses to begin using. It gives both you and the critic a chance to gain equilibrium and to get control of your emotions.

Critic: "Your report did not satisfy the requirement."

Response: "Chris, which requirement do you mean?"

To profit the most from criticism while protecting yourself, you need a strategy for long-term response. In reflection, determine the importance of the criticism. Does it justify your attention? Weigh the pros and cons of change. If you want to take action on it, ask yourself how much energy must be invested. Plan to make the necessary changes. These four strategies will help:

1. Make a written contract with yourself. Actually state in writing what you are going to do and when you will start. Sign your name, just as if you were signing a contract. Make sure that the behavior you describe is something you can and will do.

2. Decide what changes must be made. What elements or factors are involved in the change? Break them into manageable tasks. For example, if you want to improve your voice quality when responding to criticism, practice your response with a tape recorder. Listen to the tape, and evaluate your voice. Are the intonations smooth and positive? Think about how your response could be improved, and record the appropriate changes. Once you believe you have perfected your response on tape, play it for two or three friends and ask for their evaluation. Make any necessary changes. Once you have perfected your response on tape, say it in unison with the recording until it seems natural to you.

3. Build some penalties into your practices or procedures that will flag you down, or create some distances that make it harder to continue with the criticized behavior. For example, our workshop participants ask five colleagues to inform them if they are or are not doing what they contracted to do. Anyone would rather be told they are doing right, so having put themselves "on the spot," the participant tries harder and is more often successful.

4. Think of the reward you will gain by changing your behavior. You may become a model of maturity for others in your group. You could positively influence an entire work group. Colleagues will become more likely to trust you and tell you what they *really* think about other matters.

How can I respond to criticism so that both the person criticizing and I profit, and our relationship grows? More important than set rules or formulas is the spirit in which criticism is offered and accepted. Criticism can be a positive form of emotional support, a step to growth, productivity, satisfaction, and fulfillment. You will receive criticism for the rest of your life. No one enjoys it, but it is a vital tool for personal growth. The effective listener learns how to profit from it. This also is part of the Language of Effective Listening.

Emotions, like fire, can burn or warm. You decide if you will be warmed or burned by choosing how you will respond. You may have been burned by painful experiences and words. You may have been singed by untimely or inappropriate feelings. So you may try to bury your emotions, but the coals will not be extinguished, and they can flare up when least expected. When fire is under control it is a valuable friend. You will never be without emotions that can warm or burn.

Chapter Nine

Communisuasion: How to Listen Persuasively

It is almost impossible to change a person's belief system or preferences without that person's permission!

—A. K. Robertson

Contrary to popular belief, it is the effective listener, not the speaker, who often controls the conversation. Listening can be a powerful persuasion technique. Every emotion and every thought seek a companion. The need for communion is so strong that the speaker will often bond with the listener who provides this companionship and follow the leading question or probing response. By asking appropriate questions and responding in a way that reflects the thoughts, feelings, and mannerisms of the speaker, the listener can often steer the thoughts of the speaker. To be an effective "persuader," the listener must first prove himself or herself trustworthy.

My associate, Dr. Don Osgood, and I coined a word and a workshop to explain, illustrate, and teach these concepts. The word is *communisuasion*™, composed of two words, *communis*, understanding, and *suasion*, influence with integrity. The effective listener knows the skill of communisuasion, that is, how to understand the client and influence with integrity. Much depends on the listener.

BUILD TRUST

Trustworthiness is invaluable to a person's overall success. A 20-year study at Harvard University by Dr. Robert Coles established that the single most important way to ensure the success of your children is to teach them high moral values. The Forum Corporation researchers chose 341 salespeople from 11 companies representing five different industries. Of those 341, 173 were high-performance professionals, and 168 were moderate producers. The salespeople had equal knowledge and ability. What separated the high performers from the moderate ones? Trust made the difference. The high performers were believed to be most trustworthy.

Donald Seibert, former chief executive officer and chairman of the board of J. C. Penney Company, Inc., says, "Among the people I know at the top of the nation's major corporations, the personal quality that is regarded most highly is a solid, unwavering sense of integrity. The higher a person moves up in business, the more important it is for his peers and superiors to feel they can depend on his word. They have to know that he's a 'straight shooter' in every sense of the word, one who won't cut moral corners to further his own interests."

Senior managers agreed that after "concern for results," the most important trait that enhances executive success is integrity. More than 66 percent of those questioned listed this quality as a key executive characteristic.[1]

Fred Clarkson's Boston Challenge provides a more homey illustration of the value of trust. Fred claimed that he could sell more $5 bills for $10 than traditional salesmen could sell $10 bills for $5. Each man was allowed 20 attempts. That evening on the streets of Boston, Fred sold six $5 bills for $10, while his competition sold only two $10 bills for $5. The six buyers who obviously made poor purchases were asked why they bought $5 bills for $10. All six stated that they knew it was a poor trade, but something inside of them said it was the right thing to do. Eighteen who refused to pay $5 for a $10 bill, when asked why they passed up such a good deal, admitted that it was an excellent trade, but they opposed the manipulative techniques of the salesperson.[2]

You may be convinced that the listener's response to the speaker will determine the speaker's response to the listener, but you may find it difficult to act on that belief in real experience. When the speaker's characteristics, subject matter, or emotionally laden words are distasteful, it is difficult to be nonjudgmental. Without saying a word or even realizing what you are doing, you can distance yourself from the speaker with your nonverbal responses.

To assure the speaker that you are trustworthy requires flexibility. The more unlike the persuadee you are, the more flexible you will need to be to gain that person's trust. The more like the person you are, the greater the likelihood you will be trusted.

GAIN RAPPORT

When you don't have rapport, tension is increased. You need to consciously *identify* the unique behavior patterns of the person you want to influence. Once you identify the characteristics, and you are flexible and *reflect* this pattern to the speaker, tension is reduced. The speaker is more likely to accept your suggestions in a relaxed atmosphere. When properly applied, this technique of reflection builds trust and earns you the chance to prove yourself. Keep in mind, however, that it is not necessary and it may be dangerous to try to mirror the speaker exactly.

Both parties in a conversation should be looking out for the other's best interests. "To communicate on the level of real persuasion—not the seductive, deceptive, or manipulative persuasion forms ... requires a fuller appreciation of the other's values, views, priorities, basic beliefs, and goals. Persuasion is a co-active process, in which both profit. There must be a benefit to both the persuader and the persuadee."[3] You will not want to sell an idea or product that is wrong for the person; such a transaction will come back to haunt you.

Product knowledge, although important, is not the primary key to sales. "Eighty percent of the knowledge prerequisite to effective sales is about human behavior, particularly the behavior of your client."[4]

For persuasion to be a win/win situation, the persuader needs to:

Identify

Reflect

Suggest

The process of understanding the persuadee is significantly enhanced when the persuader encourages the pursuadee to talk. Talking can be easily encouraged by some timely, probing questions. Questions can be used to identify both the styles and needs of the pursuadee. As the pursuadee shares information, the informed listener will *identify* the following categories or patterns of behavior:

1. The speaker's body language.
2. The speaker's primary motivation.
3. The speaker's sorting pattern.
4. The speaker's preferred sensory mode.

Identify the Speaker's Body Language

Much nonsense written about body language has convinced some that they can become instant experts and omnipotent persuaders after reading a few pages from a popular paper-back. Nonverbal communication is more than what is popu-larly known as *body language*. In-depth study of nonverbal communication has revealed hundreds of thousands of dif-ferent ways the body speaks, necessitating a whole new set of words to describe the findings: terms like *proxemics*, the study of space and how people use and relate to it; *paralin-guists*, the study of all cues in oral speech other than the content of the words spoken; *allokines*, the smallest units of analysis of body movements; and *allophones*, the smallest units of analysis of human speech.

Nonverbal communication includes the study of "pos-ture and facial expressions, but many other things as well. [It includes] the inflection and quality of the voice, the distance between speakers and listeners, the messages con-veyed by the way a speaker chooses to clothe or decorate the body, the method a speaker uses to decide when it is his or her turn to talk, and so on."[5]

The topic of nonverbal communication is discussed in greater depth in the next chapter. The following highlights key areas a listener should be alert to.

Elements of Body Language

Be aware of all changes in body language. Albert Mehrabian reports that the body projects the thoughts and feelings of the mind and will visibly convey about 55 percent of the speaker's meaning. Sigmund Freud said, "He that has eyes to see and ears to hear may convince himself that no mortal may keep a secret. If his lips are silent, he chatters with his fingertips; betrayal oozes out of him at every pore."[6]

The speaker's voice. The way the words are said, Mehrabian concluded, will give you about 37 percent of the meaning being conveyed. Is the voice harsh, soft, loud, nasal? What is the volume, rate, pitch? You will not mirror distasteful elements, but it is helpful to be aware of offensive elements, noticing if they are constant or intermittent.

The speaker's facial expression.   The face reveals a major part of the speaker's attitude and feelings. Meaning is read in the face (see next chapter). Poker players practice maintaining the same facial expression throughout the game. The poker face is worn so that no clues to the player's hand are given.

The speaker's eyes.   Eyes have been called the windows of the soul. We are aware of communication coming from the eyes. "If looks could kill, he'd be dead" is one telling example of such messages. It is difficult for most speakers in our culture to control their eyes to hide their attitude. Observe the direction of eye movement, up, down, to the side. Are the eyes focused directly toward you or away? Among Anglos, increased eye contact usually means increased comfort and trust. Some cultures consider prolonged eye contact rude.

The speaker's proxemic zone.   How close does the speaker want to be to you? In North America, about four feet or more is usually a comfortable business distance. If the listener is too close or too far away, the speaker is uncomfortable but usually doesn't know why. Be aware of whether or not the speaker would like for you to be closer or farther away. We may violate proxemics by missing the speaker's preference.

Verbal proxemics.   Just as the listener can be too close or too far away from the speaker physically, so that person can be too close or too far away verbally. Become aware of how formal or informal your language should be. Familiarity breeds contempt. Let the speaker set the pace. Don't intrude on the speaker's mental space.

Contact or no contact.   Some speakers will want to touch or pat a listener. Is it a friendly touch of an associate? Or is it an "overly friendly" pat or the stiff pointed finger of an antagonist? Others will choose not to have any physical contact. Become aware of the preference of the one you are listening to.

Territorial rights. The speaker will have a close identification with certain objects and specific locations. Observe the degree of possessiveness regarding office, pen, pencil, and so forth.

The speaker's body stance. Observe the speaker's posture. Is it sitting or standing, rigid or relaxed, leaning forward or back, displaying interest or involvement, or positioned back and away, demonstrating reluctance?

The speaker's gestures. How often does the speaker gesture? Are the gestures relaxed and confident or emphatic and concerned? Are they big and broad, demonstrating emotional involvement, or small and constrained, showing the speaker exercising great care?

Body Language Checklist

❏ Speaker's voice.
❏ Speaker's facial expression.
❏ Speaker's eyes.
❏ Speaker's proxemic zone.
❏ Verbal proxemics.
❏ Contact?
❏ Territorial rights.
❏ Speaker's body stance.
❏ Speaker's gestures.

Recognize the Speaker's Primary Motivation

At any given time, the speaker may have a primary or umbrella motivation under which all other motives dwell as subordinates. Some primary motives are productivity, power, and relationships.[7] With probing questions and astute listening you may discern the speaker's primary motivation. Motivated by *productivity*, a person is driven by what can be accomplished, how much can get done or be "made to happen." The one motivated by *power* seeks personal autonomy or control over circumstances. The individual wants "ownership" of job responsibilities and personal life. The individual motivated by *relationships* with people is most concerned about how others may feel, think, and react to decisions. Careful listening will frequently provide this information. Can you identify the motivation of the people with whom you are developing improved communication?

Identify the Speaker's Sorting Pattern

People process information in their own way and for their own purposes. At any given moment, an individual will be acquiring information consciously or unconsciously for protecting a position or possessions or preventing failure. Listen well. Is the speaker defensive, tentative, or confident in talking about the subject?

Identify the Speaker's Preferred Sensory Mode

John Grinder and Richard Bandler have demonstrated that each of us has a primary sense by which we prefer to learn and to enjoy life. This sensory system—either sight, sound, feeling, smell, or taste—is supported by the other modes. Identify the speaker's preferred sensory system. You discover it not by talking but by listening.

Sales experts claim that, in the United States, about 80 percent of the population prefer the "show me" system.[8] When we see it, we "get it." Our next system of understanding in the United States is hearing. Recently, more attention has been paid to touch, taste, and smell. Smell and taste seem to be more rare as preferred systems than the first three. Often they are treated as a single system, because physiologically they are closely connected.

We can identify the speaker's preferred sensory mode by listening to the classification of words that person uses. Examples of the seeing mode are "I see what you mean," "that's clear," "the outlook is speculative," or "I foresee." Seeing words are easy to recognize. Hearing words such as "that rings a bell," "you are coming through loud and clear," and "that sounds good to me, we are in tune," are also easy to discern and are used most often by those who prefer to learn, understand, and live through the hearing mode.

Those who prefer to rely on the feeling or touch mode might say, "That is easy to grasp," "it's an uphill climb from here," "it flows well," or "that's a hot idea."

One who prefers the smelling mode might say, "That situation stinks," "he came out of it smelling like a rose," or "let's sniff around and see what we can find." Perfume testers have developed this sense. Nonsighted professionals in my workshops claimed to identify colleagues by smell. It may be that when one sense is lost or diminished, we tend to rely more heavily upon the others. Interestingly, the sense of smell has the strongest memory component and can be used to recall situations that seemed beyond memory. In a flash, the smell of an object once familiar to us can catapult us back in time.

Examples of the use of the taste mode would include expressions such as, "That deal leaves a bad taste in my mouth," "I feel sick about the situation," "I can almost taste victory now," or "it was a real sweet shot." Wine tasters have developed this sense more than most.

Every word will not fit into one of the five sensory modes. Words such as think, decide, deliberate, and indicate, for example, are all nondescript words. If the speaker uses such words, you will want to respond in a similar mode. If you are uncertain of the speaker's mode, use nonspecific words.

To heighten your awareness of the various sensory preference indicators, make a list of words that you hear and place them in the various sensory categories.

DISCOVER YOUR PREFERRED SENSORY MODE

Discovering your own preferred sensory category will also be insightful. Whether you prefer a visual, auditory, or feeling-action mode is largely a matter of conditioning.[9] You can increase your level of awareness and decide if you have a preference by answering the following two sets of questions. Perhaps none of the options are what you would normally say. That's OK. Just pick the one that you would use if you had to use one of them. Place a check by your choice and add up your totals. One choice is in seeing mode, one in hearing mode, one in feeling/touch mode, and one does not use any of the sensory modes.

Set One

1. Your boss has called a meeting to determine if you think it would be fair for you to rearrange your vacation time to accommodate an overly demanding customer. The deal is unfair to you. You will be asked to express your frank opinion. What will you say?

   a. It's clear to me that it would be unfair to have to change my vacation plans at this date.

  b. It sounds to me like it would be unfair for me to
     have to change my vacation plans.

  c. I feel that it would be unfair for me to have to
     change my vacation plans at this time.

  d. I don't think that it would be fair for me to have
     to change my vacation plans at this time.

2. The departmental planning session is going
   nowhere. You know that any more time spent in
   this way will be totally wasted. You want to speak
   up, but you want to be diplomatic. What would
   you say?

   a. It isn't clear to me what's missing, but I believe
      we are overlooking some important points.

   b. I can't tell exactly what they are, but it sounds to
      me like some important points have been left
      unspoken.

   c. I don't yet have a grasp of what we need, but I
      feel that we have the resources within this
      group to pull things together.

   d. It seems to me that we are missing some key
      concepts that are necessary to a satisfactory
      resolution.

3. You recognize that you have made a serious
   mistake in judgment, and now you are being called
   on the carpet for it. How would you admit your
   mistake?

   a. You're right, it looks like I made a mistake on
      this one.

   b. You're right, it sounds like I made a mistake on
      this one.

   c. I feel that you are right, I made a mistake on this
      one.

d. You're right, I believe I made a mistake on this
one.

4. You are trying to lose weight and are having some
success. Your associates express disagreement with
your diet. How would you respond to their
criticism?

a. You can see that the diet works. Take a look at
the scale—seeing is believing.

b. The diet speaks for itself. I lost 10 pounds; it
works.

c. I feel much lighter and don't get as tired as
easily as I used to. The diet works.

d. I think the point is obvious. The scale proves the
diet is effective.

5. The rumor mill is disparaging the character of a
colleague. You know the rumor is false. When an
associate tells you the rumor as if it were true, what
would you say to set the record straight?

a. I have a different point of view. Take a look at
the facts, and you'll see that the rumor is false.

b. I have heard what really happened. Listen to the
facts; the rumor is false.

c. I feel that I have the truth. When you get hold of
the facts you'll know the rumor is false.

d. I know the facts in this case and believe you will
judge the rumor false when you understand
them.

Set Two

1. You are going to learn a new job skill. Which of the
following options would you choose?

a. Learn by listening to a tape with an instructor.

    b. Learn by watching a videotape with an instructor.

    c. Learn by "walking through" the instruction with an instructor.

2. You are going to choose a recreational activity. Which one would you choose? One that:

    a. Primarily uses your eyes?

    b. Primarily uses your ears?

    c. Primarily uses your hands?

3. Close your eyes and think about the interior of the first car that you ever owned. Now, if you were to describe the interior, how would you do it? What words help you to remember it best?

    a. Words that describe how the dashboard looked?

    b. Words that describe how the seats felt?

    c. Words that describe how the radio sounded?

Practice Identifying the Speaker's Preferred Sensory Mode

Just as you can identify your own preferred sensory mode in different situations, you can identify the preferred mode of the speaker. You want to create flexibility in yourself to be able to change from your preferred mode to the sensory mode of the speaker if they are different.

1. Listen to radio and TV interviews and practice trying to identify the categories of the speakers.

2. Watch movies and again practice identifying categories.

3. Listen closely to your family members and friends. Can you identify a preferred sense?

4. Finally, practice identifying the preferred mode of someone you work with.

ILLUSTRATION 9–1
Effective Listeners Are Conscious of the Speaker's Nonverbal Communication

After a few weeks of consciously trying to identify sensory modes, you will begin to do it unconsciously.

When you have identified the speaker's body language, primary motivation, sorting pattern, and preferred sensory mode, you can reflect them back to the speaker. Reflect any mannerism, style, or observed characteristic that is not a negative idiosyncrasy. For example, if the speaker's arms are crossed, you may subtly cross your feet. If the speaker is more concerned about maintaining positive relationships with associates than with increasing productivity, you will want to demonstrate how you and your service or product may encourage positive relationships. The speaker may be more concerned about *not failing* than about being successful or vice versa. That invites you to suggest how to meet this need. When possible, of course, use words from the speaker's preferred sensory mode throughout the discussion. As much as possible, listen more than you talk! Try to do so at the same rate, pitch, and volume as the speaker.

Remember, people judge others by their own standards. The more flexible you are, the more effective you will be as a persuader.

To ensure your success, observe these cautions:

1. If you already have rapport, keep it, don't change a thing. "Don't fix it if it ain't broken." *Do* cautiously reflect some of the nonverbal communication of the speaker to gain rapport.

2. Work on reflecting one mannerism or style at a time.

3. Reflect a similarity of the speaker, posture, gesture, voice, eye movements, but do not mimic the speaker. Don't give the speaker the idea that you are strange or that you are making fun. Again, be careful.

4. Practice with "training wheels" by watching TV talk shows or similar programs. Turn off the sound and by nonverbal communication try to pick up on what is being said. Choose one character and practice carefully reflecting that person.

Reflecting is "speaking the language" of the other person so that you are understood. If you have ever had great trouble communicating with another person, it was probably because you were not speaking the same language, even though you may have used the same words. Milton Erickson coined the term *pacing* to refer to "meeting the other person where he or she is, reflecting what he or she knows or assumes to be true, or matching some part of his or her ongoing experience."[10]

When we have rapport, the process of reflecting or pacing is often unconscious. "In moments of great rapport, a remarkable pattern of nonverbal communication can develop. Two people will mirror each other's movements—dropping a hand, shifting their bodies at exactly the same time. This happens so quickly that without videotape or film replay one is unlikely to notice the mirroring. But managers can learn to watch for disruptions in this mirroring because they are dramatically obvious when they occur. . . . Instead of smooth mirroring, there will be a burst of movement, almost as if both are losing balance. Arms and legs may be thrust out and the whole body posture changed in order to regain balance."[11]

FLEXIBILITY IN YOUR CORNER

Much depends on flexibility. "Style flex" is the temporary adjustment of one individual to another to work more effectively together and to be understood.[12] This flexibility can be attained without losing your own integrity or naturalness. "Women are far better at observing body language and using it effectively than men are."[13] Men beginning our training have expressed the fear that they might lose their individuality by getting in sync with another person, but individuality need not be sold at the expense of understanding. Those with the greatest flexibility or a "requisite variety" of responses will be most successful. The best salespeople appear to be most like their customers without compromising their integrity in any way.

"The more two individuals share movement or posture together, the greater the rapport between them. Such rapport contributes to a sense of acceptance, belonging, and well-being."[14] This synchronization is a powerful communicator at the subconscious level. A smile is a universal language, and so is reflecting or pacing the speaker. When two people are effectively communicating, their bodies show it. "An eyelid blinks or a finger curls in synchrony with a particular word, sound, or voice stress."[15]

This phenomenon is readily seen in videotapes of workshop participants doing effective listening exercises. As participants gain rapport, they unconsciously swivel in their chairs, rock, scratch, blink, smile, and make countless other movements in synchrony. They synchronize, and they are unaware that they are moving together! I watched a

200-pound, six-foot one-inch black man from New York City synchronize with a 100-pound, five-foot-tall white woman from Georgia. In contrast, I have seen two men or two women of similar backgrounds in disharmony.

Reflecting on past and present. It may be possible to reflect or pace by identifying some historical agreement with the pursuadee. If something in your past agrees with the past of the speaker, share that similarity. Did you go to the same school or live in the same state? Is there something in the present upon which you have agreement? It's really easy to find things in common if you are willing to take a little initiative.

Reflect the speaker's feelings. Recognize if the persuadee is sad, angry, surprised, fearful, disgusted, or happy, and reflect a similar emotion on your face and in your voice. For example, if a customer calls and is irate about a faulty product, late appointment, improper charge, or other problem, show your concern by also being irate, not about the customer, but about the error. If you do this, your customers will know that you understand how they feel. Do observe this caution: you need not accept culpability for the error now. You are merely establishing that you know a problem exists.

Customer: "We asked that the product be delivered *next* month, and it's already here. Our warehouse is *overstocked*, and you guys will want to bill us 30 days *ahead* of our schedule. *What* went wrong?"

Response: "That's terrible. You wanted the product *next* month and it's already arrived at an *overstocked* warehouse and started a billing process 30 days *ahead* of schedule. I'll talk with shipping and find out *what* went wrong and get back to you."

The problem has not been resolved, but the first appropriate step was taken. Speak the language of the customer's feelings. Matching the mood brings agreement; mismatching moods brings disharmony, distance, and blurred understanding.

Reflect the persuadee's body language. If we consciously pace the mannerisms we recognize, the subconscious mannerisms follow. When interpreting body language, take care to read clusters. No single movement should be considered a definitive statement about the persuadee without other elements backing it up. For example, a person may have crossed arms, a stance interpreted by some experts to mean that person is closed minded and defensive. However, that person may be cold, tired, or have a sore arm, and may not be defensive at all. But if the person has crossed arms, continually shakes the head on a horizontal axis and tends to turn away from you, you do not have rapport!

Reflect the speaker's breathing. In Japan, at the beginning of some "quality circle" meetings, all participants breathe in unison. This unison breathing "establishes a climate of agreement and harmony . . . Studies show that as these meetings get under way, the executives in attendance bypass small matters and concentrate on important issues."[16] The astute listener can often observe the heaving chest, the rise and fall of the shoulders, or the stomach of the persuadee, and identify the breathing pattern.

Pacing the person's voice. Some top salespeople have gone to acting school to learn how to speak with different accents to sound like others without mimicking them. Your voice is a most powerful tool for reflecting the mannerisms of the persuadee. *Voice quality* is a mysterious thing. It involves pitch, nasality, volume, breathiness, harshness, and timbre. *Timbre* is that mysterious quality that tells you that the instrument you hear being played is a violin, not a flute or a piano.[17] You are capable of adjusting your voice to a likeness of almost any other human being.

As you reflect the mannerisms of the persuadee, you will find that person likes to be with you and wants to communicate with you. A trust bond has been established. Now is your opportunity to prove your trustworthiness by making *suggestions* that, from your knowledge of the speaker and your background, experience, values, knowledge, and feelings, would be proper for the persuadee. This response is dealing with the persuadee like a client instead of a statistic.

Suggesting. If your purpose of communication is only to gain rapport, your communication may only include identifying and reflecting. But if you are interested in sharing something of yourself, knowledge of your product, or an idea for the mutual benefit of yourself and another person, *suggestions* are appropriate. Milton Erickson called suggestions at this stage of persuasive listening *leading*. Leading is the process by which you help clients bridge from where they are to where you are. You can call somebody over to where you are, or you can drag them there. But nobody wants to be controlled. People want the right to make their own decisions, even if their conclusion is wrong and yours is right. They want and deserve the freedom to choose.

People tend to hire people that are like themselves. We tend to marry someone of the same body type. We like people who are like us and find it difficult to disagree with people we like. Consequently, the better you are at pacing, the more influence you have. If you truly reflect the mannerism, thoughts, and feelings of the speaker, you reflect that individual's inner life and will naturally begin to empathize. The result is that you will often intuitively know when to make verbal suggestions. A moral imperative is to be true to that empathy and be as transparent to the pursuadee as that person has been to you. The suggestions you make need to be in line with your understanding of what the persuadee needs and wants.

Anthony Allesandra compared traditional sales methods with nonmanipulative, client-oriented presentation.

To meet people in the areas of their need and understanding is what the Apostle Paul had in mind when he said,

ILLUSTRATION 9–2
Contrast in Selling Styles[18]

Traditional Selling	versus	*Nonmanipulative Selling*
Salesperson oriented		Client oriented
Creates needs		Discovers needs
"Talks at" client		"Discusses with" client
Makes sales		Makes customers
Inflexible		Adaptable
Increases fear and distrust		Increases trust and understanding

"I have become all things to all men in order that I might win some."

Before you make your suggestion, check to see if you have rapport. If you make a movement and your persuadee follows with a similar movement, you are in the enviable yet responsible position of being able to make a suggestion that has the highest probability of being accepted, all other things being equal.

If effective listeners work at communisuasion, they will be given the privilege and responsibility of powerful influence over those with whom they communicate. The influence will grow as long as the listener is faithful to the integrity of this skill and makes those suggestions that are congruent with the values of life.

Chapter Ten

Sharpen Your Nonverbal Skills

As a man thinks in his heart, so is he.

—Hebrew Proverb

Learning is acquired by reading books, but the much more necessary learning, the knowledge of the world, can only be acquired by reading men, and studying all the various editions of them.

—Lord Chesterfield, "Letters to His Son"

Up to 90 percent of what a person communicates is sent nonverbally through posture, facial expressions, gestures, tone of voice, and many other factors. Subconsciously, you understand nonverbal communication and respond to it with nonverbal communication of your own. When the boss says, "Nice job," but his voice is less than enthusiastic, you rightly conclude that it wasn't a nice job. The slope of your shoulders and the bend in your neck communicate that you understand. When a white, middle-class American is unable to look at you during at least part of your conversation, you conclude that the person is uninterested. Many of the interpretations of nonverbal communication lie in the subconscious.

To get a complete message you must attend to the nonverbal as well as the verbal communication of the speaker. As you do so you learn more of the Language of Effective Listening, and you grow in conscious awareness of what the speaker is communicating.

LISTENING WITH THE WHOLE BODY

We constantly send nonverbal messages, consciously or otherwise. We cannot *not* communicate. When you pay attention to the speaker, fully concentrating on what is said, your body speaks more positively. Your responsive body language can have a profound effect on the speaker. A listener provides the speaker with almost constant feedback that the listener is or is not paying attention. This feedback includes information about the level of the attention. When the listener is most attentive, the body actually moves in time and intensity with the speech of the speaker.[1]

Six students were trained by psychologists Allen Ivey and Eugene Oetting in *attending behavior*, the ability to concentrate on the speaker. As an experiment, the students attended a class to observe the effect of their nonverbal communication on the lecturer. The students began with nonattending classroom behavior, and the professor, unaware of their plan, methodically read his notes without gestures. At a predetermined signal, the students all began to attend, and the professor perked up. Within 30 seconds he gave his first gesture, his speech speeded up, and the class took on new life. Simply by physically showing that they were interested, the class was changed. Then the students stopped attending. The teacher, after an awkward attempt to engage the students, resumed the deliberate lecture with which he started the class.[2] This experiment in "whole body listening" demonstrates the potential power of the listener.

To influence the speaker in a positive way or even fully understand the speaker, the listener must carefully attend to the nonverbal cues of the speaker. All nonverbal communication must be interpreted within a context. On one occasion, the client's legs were crossed, toes pointing directly at the salesperson. The salesperson interpreted this as positive interest. In another context, when the client's toes were pointing away, the salesperson interpreted the posture as a sign of lack of interest. What the salesperson didn't know was that the individual in the second scene had an injured foot and had to keep it immobile and pointing in a direction that happened to be away from the salesperson. Nonverbal communication must be interpreted in clusters. No single nonverbal cue stands alone. Crossed arms may be a sign of defensiveness or being closed to the speaker, but if this signal is not backed up by a facial expression that expresses rejection, you cannot be sure of its meaning.

The way to learn the meaning of nonverbal communication is to reflect the nonverbal communication of others. Imitate the mode you observe, and ask yourself how you feel and what it means. TV actors and commentators can serve as models for you. Watch TV with the sound turned off and note the person's posture, gestures, and facial expressions. Then imitate them. If your body reflects that of the TV personality, and the person on the screen is depicting a character from your culture, your body will teach you what is being said.

If you have a VCR, videotape several segments of characters you will model. After you have viewed the segments without sound and practiced reflecting the nonverbals, turn on the sound. Ask yourself if the verbal communication synchronizes with the nonverbals. Practice using the same tone, speed, and pitch of the voice. Reinforce your learning by writing it down.

After you have had significant practice with the TV, begin modeling the nonverbals of people in your environment. As you observe them, ask yourself what they are thinking and feeling. It may take many months, even years, to understand the nonverbals in your environment, but the payoff will be worth the effort.

When verbal and nonverbal communication seem to contradict each other, believe the nonverbal communication. Actions speak louder than words. Think about a time when you were afraid and didn't want to show it. Although you attempted to calm your voice, your lip was trembling, and you may have been shivering. Your body gave you away.

What is true of nonverbal communication in your culture may not be true of another. Facial expressions are universal, but gestures are not. Burping after a good meal was a sign of satisfaction and gratitude in the Mongolian culture but a sign of crudeness and bad manners in the United States. Standing within a foot of a business associate in Brazil may be required to show interest, but it is intrusive in the United States.

The more attentive you are to the speaker and the more you consciously try to mirror the body language, the more likely it is that your entire body will synchronize with the speaker, helping you to understand what is being said. Recently developed high-speed cameras have picked up something the naked eye could not see. An attentive listener unconsciously mimics the physical movements of the speaker within 50 milliseconds of the speaker's movements. An effective speaker is like an orchestra conductor.[3]

NONVERBAL CUES CATALOG

On the following pages you find a catalog of nonverbal cues. Review the catalog to develop an increased awareness of what to pay attention to. The catalog provides a series of suggestions to get you started in your observations. (The list cannot be exhaustive, because the number of cues and combinations of cues is almost infinite.)

Review the nonverbal categories. To reinforce your learning, come back to the list and record your observations while viewing one or more TV characters from your culture. You have had a lifetime of assimilating nonverbals, and subconsciously you know what many of them mean. "What you learn from is the feedback you get from your own body as you try to match the body language being demonstrated. ... No set of detailed written instructions will replace the feedback you get from your body," writes Dr. Elgin.[4] This exercise will raise to the conscious level the information that is buried in past experience. So while you reflect nonverbal cues, ask your body what it is saying. For more help, keep the catalog in front of you while practicing with the TV. After some practice with the TV, you will be more aware and better able to interpret the cues sent by the five persons with whom you are trying to improve communication.

Remember the two cardinal rules: (1) All cues need to be interpreted in context and in clusters. No single cue is sufficient to determine its own meaning. No cue can be correctly interpreted out of context. (2) If you accurately model the nonverbal cues from your native culture and ask yourself what they mean, you will gain a conscious understanding of them.

Cues Using Time

In my early years of teaching workshops, I wasn't as aware of nonverbal communication as I am now. If, midway through the morning, I saw someone glance at a watch or clock, that usually didn't bother me. Even if a man stared at his watch I wasn't bothered. Not until he took off his watch and shook it did I realize it was time for a coffee break![5]

Cues to observe.
1. Promptness or delay in recognizing the presence of another or in responding to the communication.

2. A glance at a clock or ignoring any reference to time.
3. Amount of time one is willing to spend communicating with a person. Note relative amounts of time spent on various topics.
4. Preference for or aversion to a time of day, week, or month.

Now turn on the TV and observe a character with the sound off. Is any reference to time evident in the nonverbals? Note the cluster of accompanying nonverbal cues. If you recognize what you believe are relevant nonverbals related to time, mirror the behavior and ask yourself what it means.

Description of observation. _____

Meaning of nonverbal cue(s). _____

A second observation. _____

Meaning. _____

Gesturing

All normally organized human beings gesture while they are talking. In some people, the movement may be so slight it goes unnoticed. In others, it may be emphatic and be misinterpreted.

* * * * *

Jerry Wendslow was the town pharmacist. Everyday he walked between his home and the drugstore. He saved a great deal of time by taking a short cut through the local cemetery. One night in early autumn, after filling a record number of prescriptions, Jerry finally headed home. Clouds obscured the moon. Fog blanketed the ground. He never noticed the grave that had been dug that afternoon. Jerry fell in.

He tried to climb out, but the grave was deep, and the ground was soft. His efforts were futile. He cried out, but nobody within the sound of his voice had functioning ears.

After 30 minutes he gave up the struggle and resigned himself to await the arrival of the burial party the next morning. Curling up in the corner of the grave, he fell sound asleep.

Two hours later, Jeb Plowman passed by the cemetery with his dog Blue. They were hunting the raccoon who had been eating the corn on Jeb's nearby farm. Suddenly, Blue spotted the culprit and chased him into the graveyard. Now Jeb was very superstitious and the last place he wanted to be was in a graveyard at midnight. But he had been hunting that raccoon for a long time. By the sound of his bark, it seemed Blue had treed that 'coon.

Jeb steeled his jaw, set his nerves, and ran after his barking hound. He bumped into six tombstones before falling into the same grave that had swallowed Jerry two hours earlier. Jeb threw down his rifle and in a panic began to scream and claw at the sides of the grave.

Jeb's screams woke Jerry. Knowing that Jeb's efforts were futile, Jerry reached out with compassion and put his hand on Jeb's shoulder. "Give it up, Jeb," Jerry advised solemnly. "You're never going to get out of here."

Three seconds later Jeb was out.

*   *   *   *   *

On occasion, a misunderstood hand gesture can be helpful. But don't count on it!

Hand and arm gestures.

1. Symbolic hand and arm gestures like "that was close" or "stop" or "come on."

2. Literal hand and arm gestures to indicate size or shape like "it was this big" or "it was square, like this."

3. Demonstration of how something happened or how to do something. For example, "To be effective in your presentation to the marketing group, stand on this side of the flip chart, face the group, and point with your left hand."

Again, observe your character on TV with the sound off. Note the gestures and accompanying nonverbals. Model the behavior and ask yourself what it means.

Description of observation. _____

Cluster of supporting cues. _____

Meaning of nonverbal cue. _____

Meaning. _____

Nonverbal signals or commands:

1. Snapping fingers.
2. Holding finger to lips.
3. Pointing.
4. Staring directly at a person.
5. Shrugging shoulders.
6. Waving.
7. Nodding of head.
8. Winking.
9. Shaking of head.

Once again, pay attention to your TV character(s) with the sound off. Are any of the above cues evident? If so, model them and ask yourself what they mean?

Description of observation. _____

Supporting cluster of cues. _____

Meaning of nonverbal cue(s). _____

Touching cues.
1. Tapping on shoulder.
2. Caress.
3. Poking of finger at another.
4. Slapping on back.
5. Pat on top of head.
6. Handshake.

Is your TV character using any of the touching cues? If so, model them and ask yourself what they mean.

Description of observation. _____

Supporting cluster of cues. _____

Meaning of gesture. _____

Posturing Cues

A soldier on Guadalcanal described his "deadly combat" with his mortal enemy as follows:

> The foxhole I found was so small I had to drop into it sideways. I woke when I felt a hand on my chest. I swung at the guy, and we rolled out of the hole. I felt him groping at my side as I stood to loosen my machete, but he wasn't making a sound. I couldn't get at my weapon, and he hit me on the hip. But there wasn't any strength behind the blow. When I felt a thousand needles penetrating my right hand, I realized what had happened—I had been attacked by my own right arm, which had fallen asleep when I lay on top of it.[6]

Asking your body what nonverbals mean is only helpful if your body is properly functioning.

Body posturing cues.
1. Leaning forward.
2. Slouching.
3. Arms crossed in front.
4. Arms crossed in back.
5. Crossing legs.
6. Seated facing other person.
7. Head down looking at floor.

With the sound of your TV turned off, try to identify any body posturing cues. The list above represents only a few cues. Model the posture, and ask yourself what your body means in that position.

Description of observation. _____

Supporting cluster of cues. _____

Meaning of posture. _____

Body distance cues. The listening workshop was presented to personnel directors with a multinational corporation from a number of different countries. I asked the director from Brazil if a distance of four feet would be appropriate for face-to-face business communication in his country. He excitedly replied, "Oh, no, that's too far away. We like to get close, like this." He leaned toward the man sitting next to him so that he was about a foot away. I then asked the man sitting next to the Brazilian director how close he liked to be in business communication. He was from Germany, and he brought the house down when he pointed at the Brazilian and said, "About six feet from *him*!"

Remember, your body knows only the nonverbal communication of your culture. So keep those TV observations focused on characters from your own culture.

1. Moves away when other moves toward.
2. Moves toward when other moves away.
3. Takes initiative in moving away or toward.
4. Distance widens or narrows gradually.

With the sound of the TV off, notice the distance between your character and other persons in the scene, model the position in your mind, imagine your body being in a similar situation. Hold yourself in a similar manner and ask yourself what it means.

Description of observation. _____

Supporting cluster of cues. _____

Meaning of observation. _____

Voice Reading Cues

Voice quality is an underrated element in the interpretation of nonverbal communication. Quality refers to the way a voice sounds as a result of such characteristics as pitch, volume, and degree of nasality. The impact of these qualities upon the listeners was graphically demonstrated by a research project on nonverbal communication by Peter Blanck and Associates. One striking finding concerned trials in which the judge knew the defendant had a record of previous felonies. By law, the jury is not allowed to know this fact unless the defendant takes the stand. The juries in these cases said they were unaware of any bias on the part of the judges, yet their verdicts were twice as likely to be guilty than in cases in which the charges were as serious but defendants had no record of felonies. "When videotapes were analyzed by independent raters, they found that the judges' tone of voice, rather than anything in their words or body movements, communicated the strongest, most negative messages."[7] Turn on your TV set, and this time watch your character with the sound on. Listen for the following voice qualities.

1. Tone of voice.
   a. Flat, monotone, absence of feeling.
   b. Bright, vivid changes of inflection.
   c. Strong, confident, firm.
   d. Weak, hesitant, shaky.
2. Rate of speech.
   a. Fast.
   b. Medium.
   c. Slow.
3. Loudness of voice.
   a. Loud.
   b. Medium.
   c. Soft.

4. Diction.
   a. Precise versus careless.
   b. Regional (colloquial) differences.
   c. Consistency of diction.
5. Pitch.
   a. High.
   b. Low.
   c. Changes in pitch.

Description of perceived voice qualities. _____
Accompany cluster of nonverbal cues. _____
Meaning conveyed by voice. _____

Face-Reading Cues

The face is the primary site for the display of feelings and nonverbal effects. In *Unmasking the Face, a Guide to Recognizing Emotions from Facial Expressions,* Paul Ekman and William V. Friesen provided research that supports and expands upon the observations of Charles Darwin. Darwin believed that facial expressions are transcultural. Ekman and Friesen confirmed this belief and analyzed how every muscle in the face works relative to each of six transcultural facial expressions. Their results provide "facial blueprints which will improve your ability to spot emotion in others and help you to be aware of what your facial muscles are saying about your feelings."[8] We now know that each of these specific facial expressions has the same meaning in Canada as it has in Japan. Facial expressions are thought by some researchers to be subject to involuntary responses.

Six basic facial expressions and their numerous combinations are revealed by three major facial areas. These expressions are surprise, fear, disgust, anger, happiness, and sadness. These expressions may appear in combinations. For example, surprise and fear or happiness and surprise may be simultaneous. They may also appear so rapidly, fleeting in a second, that to catch them you have to be looking for them.

The three major facial areas are the brow, the eyes, and the lower face. To get an accurate reading of the facial expression, you need to observe the distinctive characteristics of all three areas. You will find it easy and helpful to recognize the feelings displayed in facial expressions in photographs as you continue to practice with the TV. You can also become more aware of what your feelings are by applying this knowledge to yourself. Our feelings can be responsible for awesome success or terrible failure. Yet as Ekman and Friesen say, "We know less about our feelings than we do about our teeth, our car, or our neighbor's escapades."[9]

You will find it instructive to practice the facial expressions in a mirror. When you make an expression and ask your body what it means, you will know. The following catalog of cues helps focus your attention on the muscles that reveal the expressions of surprise, fear, disgust, anger, happiness, or sadness. Because of the explicit research done by Ekman and Friesen, we know and can share with you what each of the cues means. At the conclusion of this catalog of facial cues is an enjoyable exercise, which will test your ability to recognize combinations of expressions.

The brow cues.
1. Raised so that they are curved and high shows surprise.
2. Raised and drawn together shows fear.
3. Lowered, lowering the upper eyelid, shows disgust.
4. Skin below the brow triangulated with inner corner up shows sadness.

Using a mirror, move your brow in these ways to affirm its meaning, then pay particular attention to the brow as you observe a TV character. Model the brow of the character and ask yourself what it means.

Description of observation. _____

Supporting cluster of cues. _____

Meaning the brow is conveying. _____

Examine the eye cues. Are they:

1. Sparkling.
2. Teary.
3. Wide-eyed.
4. Is there eye contact:
    a. Looking at a specific object.
    b. Looking down.
    c. Steady at a person.
    d. Staring/glaring.
    e. Looking at other but looking away when looked at.
    f. Covering of eyes with hands.
    g. Frequency of looking at another.
5. What is the position of eyelids?

Are the eyelids wide open? Is the upper lid raised and the lower lid drawn so that the white of the eye (the sclera) shows both above and below the iris? If so, the eyes are displaying surprise.

The upper eyelid is raised, exposing sclera, the lower eyelid is tensed and drawn up. If so, the eyes are displaying fear.

1. If lines show below the lower lid, and the lid is pushed up but not tense, the eyes are showing disgust.

2. If the upper lid is tense and maybe lowered by action of the brow, the face *might* be showing anger.

3. Likewise, if the eyes have a hard stare and a bulging appearance, the eyes are *probably* displaying anger. (The entire cluster of nonverbal cues must be in place before you can be sure that the expression is one of anger.)[10]

4. If the lower eyelid shows wrinkles below it (it may be raised but not tense), the eyes are revealing happiness. If crow's-feet wrinkles go outward from the outer corners of the eyes, an additional sign of happiness is displayed.

5. When the upper eyelid inner corner is raised, the eyes are sad.

Again, use a mirror. This time, observe your various eyelid positions and affirm their meaning. Then observe a TV character, paying particular attention to the eyelids. Try to identify the meaning being conveyed.

Description of observation. _____

Supporting cluster of cues. _____

Meaning the eyelids are conveying. _____

The lower face. The lower face includes the nose, cheeks, and lips. Distinct positioning of the lips is frequently the most apparent cue in the lower face.

1. If the lower jaw is dropped open so that the teeth are parted, but there is no tension or stretching of the mouth, the person is probably surprised.

2. When the mouth is open and the lips are either tensed lightly and drawn back or stretched and drawn back, fear is evident.

3. If the nose is wrinkled, disgust is *probably* evident.

4. Raised cheeks are another sign of disgust.

5. When the lips are pressed firmly together with the corners drawn down, the person *may* be angry.

6. If the lips are open, tensed in a squarish shape as if shouting, anger is *probably* being displayed. (Unless signs of anger are seen in all three areas of the face, interpretation is uncertain.)

7. If the corners of the lips are drawn back and up, the person is happy.

8. When a wrinkle (the nasolabial fold) runs down from the nose to the outer edge beyond the lip corners, happiness is apparent.

9. When the corners of the lips are down and/or the lips are trembling, the person is sad.

Once more, use a mirror to practice identifying and affirming the various positions of the lips, nose, and cheeks. Then observe a TV character, paying close attention to the lower face. Begin by having the sound off. Are any of the above cues evident? If so, model them, and ask yourself what they mean.

Description of observation. _____

Meaning of nonverbal cues. _____

Supporting cues. _____

Now turn on the sound, and note if the facial expressions seem to fit the words and voice qualities.

Skin. Admittedly, skin is difficult to observe on TV, but you may be able to pick up some of the following. By trying to observe these cues, you will be more conscious of their presence with associates.

1. Pallor.
2. Perspiration.
3. Blushing.
4. Goose bumps.

Attempt to see any of these cues on your TV character(s). You may find it easier to concentrate on the skin if the sound is turned off. If any skin cues are evident, imagine yourself in a similar condition and ask yourself, in the context of the TV scene, what it would mean.

Description of observation. _____

Supporting cluster of cues. _____

Meaning of skin cues. _____

You have gained insight and sensitivity to nonverbal communication merely by reading through the above catalog. By doing some of the exercises, you will gain insight and experience that you won't forget. By repeating all the exercises until you are certain of what you are observing, hearing, and feeling, you will take a quantum leap in understanding the "Language of Listening." Some will find it helpful to spend a few minutes at a time on an irregular basis. Others will concentrate for half an hour or more on a regular schedule. However you do it, you will profit. The beauty of these exercises is that you can always pick up where you left off.

Face Recognition Exercise 1

The facial drawings in the following exercises were prepared by humorist Roger Petersen, who also wrote the accompanying scenario. The faces below depict one of five basic transcultural facial expressions identified by Ekman and Friesen: *happiness, sadness, fear, anger, surprise,* or *disgust.* As you read the story, "A Business Trip with the Boss," pick the word that names the facial expression. Check your answers at the end of the scenario.

* * * * *

A Business Trip with the Boss

You are flying to Denver with your boss for a two-day meeting with an important client. You are to meet him at the airport ticket counter. You arrive before he does and wait patiently. In 10 minutes you see your boss descending the escalator. As he approaches you, you compliment him on his new suit.

When you arrive to check in, the attendant tells your boss there is no record of a reservation for him.

The attendant keeps searching and eventually locates your boss's reservation. It's under your name and covers a party of two. You board the plane and take off. You both start flipping through a magazine, and your boss becomes engrossed in a photo essay on hunger conditions in India.

A half hour later, lunch is served. You ask your boss how he likes the Salisbury steak.

The pilot announces that you should be landing in Denver in about 40 minutes. Suddenly, the airplane takes an abrupt and rapid nose dive.

A few seconds later, the plane levels out and slowly gains altitude. The pilot apologizes for some unexpected air turbulence and assures a smooth ride for the duration of your trip.

How did you do? (Answers: A. Happiness, B. Anger, C. Sadness, D. Disgust, E. Fear.)

Face Recognition Exercise 2

The next exercise is a little tougher. The subtleties of facial expressions are numerous. Changes in the forehead, eyebrows, and eyelids may reflect one emotion, while the cheeks, nose, lips, and chin reveal a different one. The two emotions blend into one facial expression to show sad-angry expressions, angry-afraid expressions, surprise-fearful expressions, happy-surprise and numerous others. Even within the same emotion such as surprise, there are numerous variations.

Cover the lower part of the face on page 156 with your hand and interpret the expression in the upper part of the face. Then cover the upper part of the face to interpret the expression in the lower part of the face. Emotions depicted in faces frequently show combinations of feelings expressed so rapidly they are often missed. Very quick, "microexpressions" can reveal emotions the person is attempting to

conceal.[11] Most of the time, we miss even the "macroexpres-
sions" that can last two or three seconds, because we are not
looking at the other person.

Observe the mouth. Notice the corners of lips drawn back
and up, and a wrinkle (the nasolabial fold) running down
from the nose to the outer edge beyond each lip corner.
When either of these are evident in the facial expression,
happiness is usually present. The lower part of the face, the
mouth, depicts happiness.

Observe the upper face. The brows are raised and drawn
together. The wrinkles in the forehead are in the center, not
across the entire forehead. The upper eyelid is raised, exposing
sclera, and the lower eyelid is tensed and drawn up. The presence of these characteristics in the upper face is evidence of fear.

The combination of expressions on the first face is typical
of a person trying to conceal fear, or who is feeling both
happy and fearful at the same time (like a mother telling a
friend that her teenager just got her driver's license).

Now move on to the face above and try to recognize the combination of emotions. Again, cover the lower part of the face and observe the characteristics in the upper face. The brows are raised so that they are curved and high. The skin below the brow is stretched. Horizontal wrinkles go across the forehead. The upper eyelids are drawn back so that the white of the eye (the sclera) shows above (and below) the iris. These are characteristics of surprise.

Now cover the upper part of the face and observe the characteristics of the lower face. The mouth is similar to the mouth in the first face, the corners of the lips are drawn back and up. The only difference is that in the second figure the mouth is open, exposing the teeth. The lower face depicts happiness. This is the kind of facial blend that occurs when someone is surprised by something pleasant, such as an unexpected birthday party.

Physical Setting Cues

Space management may well be the most ignored and powerful tool for inducing culture change and speeding up innovation projects and task execution in general.

—Tom Peters

The study of space and a person's relationship to that space has become the subject of scientific investigation. Large numbers of people confined to small areas of space without appropriate safeguards produce antisocial behavior. That people in large cities surrounded by crowds are less likely to engage in casual conversation with a stranger is no coincidence. They insulate themselves to protect their privacy. Small-town residents do not share that inhibition, because their greater physical space provides them with privacy, and they can afford to be more open.

Office setting. The physical environment will either enhance or hinder effective communication. Which of the three office arrangements will be most conducive to effective communication? Why do you believe this is so?

ILLUSTRATION 10–1
Three Possible Office Settings

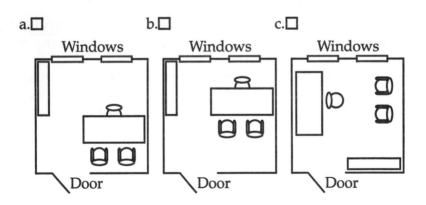

In example A, the desk is a barrier, and the two visitor chairs are pinned back against the wall. The enlarged space behind the desk chair communicates power, dominance, and control. In example B, the barriers to effective communication are modified. Example C provides the best setting for effective communication. Physical barriers are removed, and the space is equally divided.

Arrangement of the physical setting.
1. Neat, ordered, organized.
2. Untidy, haphazard, careless.
3. Casual versus formal.
4. Warm versus cold colors.
5. Soft versus hard materials.
6. Slick versus varied textures.
7. Cheerful and lively versus dull and drab.
8. Discriminating taste versus tawdry.
9. Expensive or luxurious versus shabby or Spartan.

Turn on your TV and watch until you can focus on the setting of the room. Note the arrangement of the physical setting and ask yourself what sort of feelings the elements in the room generate.

Description of the setting. _____

Feelings the setting conveys. _____

Personal dress.   A more personal element to notice in the physical setting is the person's clothing. To further increase your awareness, read one of the many books written on the subject such as *Dress for Success*. Two general categories relating to dress summarize the spectrum.

Bold versus unobtrusive.

Stylish versus nondescript.

Observe your TV characters and ask yourself what cues you would be sending if you were similarly dressed.

Description of observation. _____

Supporting cluster of cues. _____

In our final cluster of setting cues, pay attention to where the person you are observing is in relation to the setting and others in the scene. The following list will encourage your thinking, but don't stop with our list of items. They are intended only to get you started.

Position in the room.
1. Physical objects between speaker and others.
   a. Desk.
   b. Chair.
   c. Table.
   d. Other.
2. Speaker seated or standing or moving.
3. In center of room.
4. In back of room.
5. Toward front of the room.
6. In front of door or exit.
7. Speaker seated while other(s) stands.
8. Standing while other(s) sits.
9. Speaker moves toward or away from listener.
10. Listener moves toward and away from speaker.

Observe your TV character and ask yourself what the position conveys. How would you feel if you were in that position? Imagine yourself as the character in that position, and write down what you think you would feel. Imagine yourself as another in that room observing the TV personality. What would the person be conveying to you?

Observation of location and movement. _____
Any supporting cues. _____
Meaning of the position in the room. _____

Attitude-Sensing Cues

A person's attitude is unlike a feeling in that it exists for a longer time. Consequently, one's *attitude* will determine one's destiny. Most top executives concur that a positive attitude played a significant role in their success. An aware, decisive, and committed person will expect and deal productively with major problems. An attitude of frustration, defiance, or resignation, on the other hand, is known to be a hindrance to successfully dealing with even minor problems. Knowing what attitude an associate has toward an issue or person will help you be successful in the relationship.

The Osgood Attitude Curve, developed by Dr. Don Osgood after 30 years as a top internal consultant for IBM, depicts the path our feelings frequently take when we are confronted with a new situation. Finding one's position on this curve and learning to take the proper steps to move to a positive position have saved thousands of careers.

We frequently begin a new job or personal relationship *idealistically*, superficially happy and enthusiastic. Before long we realize that there is a gap between what we expected and what the situation really is. We become *frustrated*, irritated, exasperated, worried, anxious, chagrined, disappointed, and dissatisfied.

If the situation is not dealt with in a productive way, we become defiant, angry, disobedient, insubordinate, rebellious, affronting, and confrontational. We try to make the organization or relation fit our expectations. This approach encourages the downward spiral of attitude.

In the downward plunge, we lose momentum and become *resigned*, apathetic, uninvolved, passive, submissive, and accepting. This is when the "divorce" takes place in the heart and mind of the married couple, even if a legal divorce is not sought. This is when the professional has "died on the job" but is still coming to work and is counted on the payroll.

ILLUSTRATION 10–2
The Osgood Attitude Curve

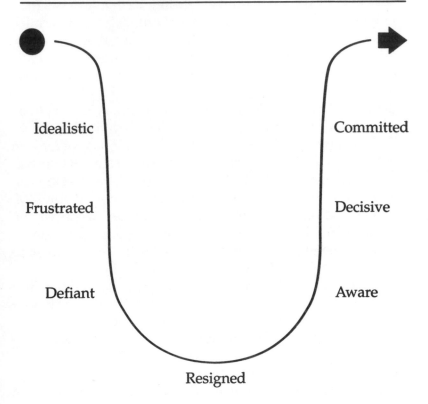

Idealistic   Committed

Frustrated   Decisive

Defiant   Aware

Resigned

Those who know the Language of Effective Listening can help themselves and others to become *aware* of what is happening. They can be open, ready for change, conscious, insightful, cognizant, appreciative of the possibilities, and even mildly surprised.

Awareness usually leads to decisiveness. The decisive first step is catalytic. With the first step you become resolved, active, resolute, and positive. From positive awareness will flow enlightened commitment. We don't expect perfection and have learned how to live with some ambiguity, but we strive for excellence. Now we become involved, internally motivated, internally coherent, and happy.

If you know what a person's attitude is, you may meet them where they are and stay in sync or lead them on to a more positive attitude. In reading attitudes it is important to read the composite of all of the sensed nonverbal cues, facial and vocal expression, gestures, posture, time cues, and the use of the setting.

Again, use your TV to practice identifying the seven attitudes. Make sure the sound is on. Pick a character and focus. Imagine yourself in the character's place, and ask yourself which of the seven attitudes you would have if you were communicating like the person you are observing.

Attitude being conveyed. _____

Cues that support this observation. _____

* * * * *

You have been reading nonverbal communication all of your life. As an infant, you babbled the full range of 70 sounds that make up the sound system of all human language.[12] From the day you were born, your body synchronized with the nonverbal communication around you. You were capable of synchronizing with and learning any of the world's languages. As you grew you discriminated, concentrating on those sounds that were uniquely used by your parents and others in your environment to express their verbal language. Your body continued to synchronize with the physical movements of the speakers around you. Your whole body learned the language. Over the years, you have added to that knowledge so that, subconsciously, you are an expert in both body language and other nonverbal communication of your culture.

Now, by consciously becoming aware of what another's body language communicates, your understanding of that communication increases up to 90 percent. A true "meeting of meanings" will come with your growing understanding of people. This greater understanding will release the potential of your relationship.

Chapter Eleven

Improve Listening through Effective Note Taking

Evidence points out that trained note takers are better listeners.

—Dr. Ralph Nichols

He listens well who takes notes.

—Dante

It is the disease of not listening, the malady of not marking, that I am troubled withal.

—Shakespeare

Note taking is an important part of our culture. I keep a pad and pencil by my telephone. I am ready to write when the phone rings. Usually, the first 15 seconds of the conversation will give the critical information, the name of the caller, and the purpose of the call.[1]

Conference tables prepared for business sessions are supplied with yellow-lined legal pads. Associates enter a manager's office equipped with pen and paper ready to take notes. Students diligently take notes in classes—and write notes to other students!

Dr. Ralph Nichols describes the frustration experienced by many note takers. "The note taker is thoroughly determined to record what he hears. The speaker starts talking, and the man with the yellow pad assumes the writing position. As the words strike his ears, he commences to write. From long experience, he knows that note taking is a tense race pitting his penmanship agility against the talker's rate of speech. Soon the man who is talking is winning the race. Good handwriting is discarded in favor of a hasty, illegible scribble. But still it's impossible to keep up with the talk. So the note taker now resorts to a telegraphic writing style with incomplete sentences and abbreviated words. Any chance this system might have had to work is lost by the time it is put into use, for the note taker has met an insolvable problem. Because he is concentrating on note taking, he has lost track of what the talker was saying. What he is hearing doesn't even make sense anymore. The telegraphic style deteriorates to doodling, which becomes the listener's main function with the note pad until the talk is finished."[2]

In about the fifth grade, we were taught to take notes by outlining and writing our papers following a specific outline.

ILLUSTRATION 11–1
Effective Listeners Know How and When to Take Notes

We began with Roman numeral I for the first main point. Capital letter *A* headed the first subpoint, Arabic 1 followed for the first subpoint under *A* and lower case *a* for the first subpoint under 1, and so forth. What we were not told is that people do not think according to this outline. To become successful in taking notes, you need to adapt your note taking to the style of the speaker's presentation. This is a form of synchronization.

WHY TAKE NOTES?[3]

You cannot concentrate on writing notes and on what the speaker is saying at the same time. In note taking you lose some of your attentiveness to the speaker. What's more, desks are covered, and drawers, cabinets, notebooks, and briefcases are filled with notes that have never been read, are inadequate, inaccurate, illegible, and incomplete. If you are an effective listener, why bother to clutter your mind and desk by taking notes?

The first important reason for taking notes is the need for a memory enhancer. Short-term memory is less than 20 seconds, and little can be done to improve it other than to learn to concentrate more fully on what the speaker is saying. However, we potentially have all the mental power necessary to remember what we need to retrieve from short-term memory. It doesn't take 20 seconds to write a skillful note.

Long-term memory, anything over 20 seconds, can be greatly enhanced by note taking. Even if you put your notes in a drawer and throw the key away but were *skilled* in the way you took your notes, you will retain more of what the speaker said, because skillful note taking engages most of your senses in processing the key elements of the message.

In note taking, you experience more of the message because your muscles are involved in writing about what you are seeing and hearing. Your eyes not only see the speaker's body language but also the words on the paper. By feeling the paper and pen, you touched what was communicated. The more senses involved in any learning process, the quicker and more complete will be the learning.

WHEN TO TAKE NOTES

Deciding when to take notes is as important as determining how to take notes. When the message is short, only a minute or two long, and the information is not worth keeping, you will only want to take notes if you find it hard to concentrate. Disciplining yourself to take skillful notes will force you to concentrate. If you are nervous, it gives you something constructive to do. By your intense concentration, you show respect for the speaker. If you can concentrate and don't need to keep the information, don't take notes.

Second, if the message is short and the information is important, keep your notes brief or write them after the message is over. The briefest notes are made with key words. If you don't take notes during the message for fear of losing something, jot down key words as soon as the message is over. The key words will give you the critical outline of the message. Fill in the details later.

Finally, when the information is confidential, taking notes may be inappropriate, even offensive or distracting to the speaker. In some situations, it may be necessary to ask the speaker's permission to take notes.

Sometimes it is not possible or practical to take notes at all while someone is speaking. For those cases, it is important to have a good knowledge of memory techniques. It also helps to listen most attentively. There is a lot of good literature available on how to concentrate.

HOW TO TAKE NOTES

When a building or any other structure is disassembled and moved to another location to be rebuilt, knowledge of the original structure is invaluable for the reconstruction. The note taker attempts to rebuild the thought structure of the speaker. If you discern the blueprint of the "structure," you are more likely to be able to reconstruct the speaker's thoughts.

Speakers have both overt and unconscious structure to their messages. The structure gives form and function to the individual's thoughts. The foundation of the speaker's point will be the main point or topic. On that main point rooms are built, ells and wings, and supporting points. The following procedure will help you build listening skill in your reconstruction projects.

Recognize the Overt Organizational Pattern:[4] Effective Listeners Follow the Speaker's Unique Organizational Structure

In today's fast-paced society, some speakers do not seem to have enough time for good organization. It's therefore important that you recognize the disorganization and make the proper adjustments. Listen for key words, concepts, and facts. When a speaker is disorganized, the effective listener listens for facts and deduces concepts.

Once you have taken the time and effort to identify a speaker's organizational pattern, you will discover a tendency to use the same structure all the time.[5] People are habitual and predictable. The best way to anticipate what a person will do tomorrow is to look at what that individual did yesterday. Which shoe do you put on first? Which leg do you put in your pants first? Which side of your face do you shave first? The content of the message does not necessarily change when a different pattern is used, only its organization changes.

ILLUSTRATION 11–2
When the Speaker is Disorganized, Effective Listeners
Listen for Facts and Deduce Concepts

Enumeration.   In the first pattern, enumeration, the speaker numbers the main thoughts. This pattern is easy to recognize and follow. Maybe that is why it is used so often in critical situations. This is what enumeration sounds like:

If you are going to be all that you are capable of being, you must take control of your future by developing three skills. (1) Be willing to give 110 percent to whatever you do. As you exert more effort, you expand your ability to accomplish even more. (2) Second, be willing to grow, to change, to learn, and to become even more than you are now. It takes courage to change. But the benefits are worth facing the fear and conquering it. (3) Be an outstanding communicator, willing to accept at least 51 percent of the responsibility for all communication in your life. If you are the speaker, you will be 51 percent responsible to make sure the listener

ILLUSTRATION 11-3
Effective Listeners Recognize and Follow the Speaker's Unique Organizational Structure

understands your thoughts and feelings. If you are the listener, you will accept at least 51 percent of the responsibility for making sure that you understand the speaker.[6]

Enumeration is easy to spot, easy to hear, and easy to follow. When taking notes, number the main points.

Problem/solution. The message organization of the problem/solution pattern is found often in business but also in personal interaction. The speaker shares a problem, lists its causes and effects, and suggests a solution. Or the speaker develops one or more of these components. The speaker may emphasize any of the elements and deemphasize the others.

For example: Here's the problem as I see it. We have hurdles to overcome if we are to become all that we are capable of being. In spite of the lack of commitment of our co-workers, if we are going to keep growing, we must hurdle the desire to conform and be willing to give 110 percent to the task. But that's not all. We also need to get over the "comfort hurdle." We tend to grow comfortable in our circumstances and unwilling to change. We need to become flexible, willing to grow and innovate while we are working toward our full potential. What can be more frustrating and difficult to hurdle than trying to listen to a

Main Points

1. _____

2. _____

3. _____

4. _____

Key Words

1. _____

2. _____

3. _____

4. _____

Principles/Concepts

1. _____

2. _____

3. _____

4. _____

co-worker who rambles on instead of getting right to the point and has an attention span of a millisecond when listening? If I am going to be everything that I can be, I've got to take at least 51 percent of the responsibility to make sure I understand that co-worker and that the co-worker understands me.

The problem/solution pattern will be easy to hear once you have tuned your ears to it. When taking notes in this pattern, you would divide your paper into problem(s) and solutions.

Time sequence.   The third universal pattern is time sequence. The speaker puts the thoughts in chronological order. Typical terms used are *hours, days, months, years*. The speaker may start in the present and progress to the future, start from the past and progress, or start from the present and regress to the past. Here's an example of the time sequence.

If you are going to be everything that you can be, you must spend the first years in your job, building the habit of giving 110 percent to the task that is before you. For some professionals, it takes several years of trial and error to learn the importance of this commitment; others never succeed and don't know why. After you have been in the job for five years and established this pattern, you need to be ready to change jobs, to grow, and to innovate.

The next 15 years on the job become the most exciting and rewarding if you are willing to change with the times. After you have been around for over 15 years, you have a senior status in many companies, and younger co-workers want to hear what you have learned. Now you have a chance to multiply your productivity through the lives of others. Accepting at least 51 percent of the responsibility for all communication in your life becomes a necessity.

When taking notes in this pattern, divide your comments according to the chronology of the message.

Spatial or pictorial organization.   In spatial or pictorial organization, the speaker draws a picture of what is communicated. The secondary organizational pattern in this message is enumeration.

Picture this: If you are going to be everything that you are capable of becoming, it is necessary that you climb your own personal ladder of success. "Give 110 percent to the job you are doing" is the first rung on the ladder. The second is the willingness to grow, to innovate, to change. The final rung is to be an outstanding communicator, accepting at least 51 percent of the responsibility for communication, whether you are the speaker or the listener.

Listen for word pictures and you will see this pattern. When taking notes, you will find it helpful to draw a picture. In our example, you would draw a ladder and label each rung appropriately.

Exercise in Recognizing Organizational Patterns

If you practice listening for these patterns, you will discover that they are relatively easy to hear. You can practice recognizing the patterns by reading the following four paragraphs and noting the primary message structure. On the space provided at the end of the paragraph put an *E* if the pattern is enumeration, *P* for problem/solution, *T* for time sequence, and *S* for spatial/pictorial. If you recognize a primary and a secondary pattern, put the primary pattern first and the secondary one second.

1. Look, we have to realize that times have changed. Fifteen years ago, if anyone got out of line, they were just thrown out in the street. We could do that because we had people in line waiting for jobs. The trouble was that union and management were at each other's throats, and the place was a mess. Today, we don't have that as much. Union and management work together better. Now the trouble is absenteeism. Ten years from now? Who knows? Maybe we won't be here tomorrow. But I can tell you, we can't go back to the old way. We have to find some way to make this thing work.[7]

Primary Organizational Pattern: _____

2. Come on, you people. You've been supervisors for 10 years. The game plan hasn't changed that much. You know what to do when something happens, just like a good lineman knows what to do because he's been coached. Don't play the hero. If you do, I'm going to penalize you. And if it keeps up, I'm going to throw you out of the game. Don't think. React. If you have to think on a football field, you're dead. You should know what to do instinctively by now. Keep working at your own job and forget about everything else.[8]

Primary Organizational Pattern: _____

3. Mary here has been having trouble with the new machine. She says it runs its cycle even when she takes her hands off of the buttons. Wayne says it can't happen. The machine is designed to stop when you take your hands off those buttons. Well, I'll tell you what's happening. Somebody has been putting some jumpers in there, and I know who it is. It's the repairmen. So somebody better talk to them.

Primary Organizational Pattern: _____

4. All right. The way I see it we have three problems. First, what to do about the absenteeism in the area. Second, what to do about the person who's stacking work up on the floor to get out early. And third, what to do about the housekeeping in the area.

Primary Organizational Pattern: _____

Speakers often use these patterns in combination and sometimes use a completely different pattern than those we have illustrated. Your goal is to identify the speaker's pattern and synchronize with the speaker's structure instead of imposing your own structure on the message. Take notes accordingly. Speakers will use the same pattern in about 80 percent of their messages, but if the message is too short, you may miss it.

Now think one more time about the Favored Five with whom you will build your communication over the next 30 days. Can you determine what pattern or combination of patterns each person prefers? Take a moment to think about it. If you can, write what you think is their pattern(s) on the line provided. Be willing to come back and reevaluate your answers after listening more closely to these individuals.

The Preferred Organizational Pattern(s)
of My Special Associates

Initials: _____   Pattern(s) _____
Initials: _____   Pattern(s) _____
Initials: _____   Pattern(s) _____
Initials: _____   Pattern(s) _____
Initials: _____   Pattern(s) _____

Identify Unconscious Message Structure

We mentioned earlier that some people best understand reality through their feelings. These kinesthetic people think or conceptualize in physical or emotional terms. They like touch and physical movement, and they understand best through feelings. When you recognize this orientation in their speech and adapt your note taking to it, you will be more effective in restructuring their thoughts.

Other individuals understand best on the conceptual level through the auditory gate, or what they hear. These are called *auditory or hearing* dominant individuals, thinking or conceptualizing in theoretical or data-based modes. They are characteristically people who are critical in the positive sense of the word. They analyze effectively. These people very often can't understand why the person who is feeling dominant doesn't share that conceptual organization. This inability to recognize and accept different patterns often results in "personality clashes" like those between McCoy and Spock on "Star Trek." When you hear this conceptual organization note in the speaker, play that tune in your notes.

The third subconscious organization is that of visual organization, thinking or conceptualizing in pictures. This individual best conceptualizes and more easily understands reality through the forming of pictures in the imagination. An example is the visionary Kirk of "Star Trek." When you see this conceptual orientation in a speaker, adjust your notes so that you are producing pictures on your paper.

Before reading about the next note-taking skill, take one second to look at each of the triangles below, and then turn the page and write what you saw in the triangles.

If you are like thousands of others who have participated in our workshops, you wrote "Paris In The Spring," "Once In A Lifetime," and "A Bird In The Hand." A hospital superintendent in one of my sessions wrote "Love Blossoms" for the first triangle, "A Golden Opportunity" for the

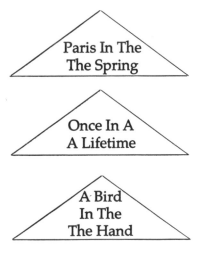

second, and "A Sure Thing" for the third triangle. Did you notice the extra *The* in the first and third triangles? The extra *A* in the second? If you did, you are unusual. Second-grade students notice the extra word because they read one word at a time. Computer programmers and editors, accustomed to working with details, also catch them. But without special training, readers continue to read only for key concepts. When listening, pay attention to the important words, the key words. They will give you the critical concepts.

Read the following statement, and list the four or five most important words giving the critical content. Then compare your list with mine.

This car will never sell. Its design is just plain ugly. And look at the price; it's way too expensive for most people. You heard about the problem with maintenance. People don't like breaking down all the time. Word gets around: this car won't sell.

Key Words _____   _____   _____

_____   _____   _____

The key words I chose are *car, won't sell, design, price,* and *maintenance.* If you got those words, you have the hooks to hang the rest of the message on. You are on target. In six words or less, you will have enough information to capture the essence of a 43-word message.

Listen for the main and supporting points. The main point in the message above is that the car won't sell. The supporting points are threefold: it's ugly, expensive, and needs too much maintenance.

Intermittent Notes

Another effective method to use with longer presentations is *intermittent notes.* The listener takes notes at appropriate intervals, possibly every couple of minutes. Most speakers are organized well enough to give you a clear idea of each main point as it is covered and provide a transition to the next point. Examples of transitional comments are, "Now I want to say" or "In addition." As you practice this note-taking skill, you will begin to identify transitions easily. The resulting notes are an abstract, sentence, or short summary of the main points that you heard. Further organization can be done later.

The intermittent note method enables the listener to maintain attentiveness for a maximum period while still providing him with sufficient notes to reconstruct the message. If the speaker is going too fast for the listener to write entire sentences, the trained note taker writes phrases or key words. A typical mistake note takers make is to try to use one method of note taking for all situations and speakers. To be successful, you need to master the various methods and be flexible in applying them.

Even if you are not taking notes physically, it is profitable to take them mentally. Remember, you think 7 to 10 times faster than the speaker is speaking. The average adult attention span is a few minutes. Your mind will wander unless you have learned and applied constructive ways to keep involved.

While the speaker is talking, be a detective. Be prepared, sense, synchronize, interpret, evaluate, and then respond. Identify the speaker's purpose, dominant sensory mode, and preferred overt and unconscious message organization. Listen for key words, and take notes when appropriate! You will learn more, and, at the same time, raise the esteem and build a relationship with the speaker.

Conclusion

The ultimate question in a book like this—the unspoken question that lurks at the back of every reader's mind—is, "Can this writer's ideas *really* change my life?"

The unequivocal answer is, *Yes, they can.* This program has proven its effectiveness in the lives of thousands of managers and professionals. One condition exists, however. If you haven't applied these ideas as you read through the text, you must begin *right now* to establish a practical action plan and then immediately put it into effect in your daily relationships. If you delay *even a day or two* the chances are that this book will become merely a brief and unremarkable interlude in an otherwise busy life.

To avoid the loss of what you've learned, take a cue from an executive named Tom. After learning the basics of listening in a seminar, he set aside the very first evening after his last class to draw up the following action plan.

Step 1: He identified five people with whom he wanted to improve his personal communications. Two were family members, including one of his children and his brother. Three were colleagues at work.

These weren't the "toughest nuts" or people who had always been nearly impossible to talk to. He would deal with the difficult ones later, after he honed his skills.

Rather, the five he picked were individuals with whom he already had a decent relationship. Yet it seemed they might draw even closer to him if he could just find ways to interact on deeper levels.

Step 2: Next, he listed specific problems he had noted in his discussions with each of these five. For example, he knew that he and a couple of people on his list always seemed to be "talking past" each other. Closer to home was that he and his child were inclined to anger one another almost every time they chatted for more than five minutes.

Step 3: Having noted the main conversational problems, Tom now began to analyze *why* each problem had developed and what he had to do to resolve it.

Take the individuals who often responded inappropriately, for example. He realized that he frequently began to interject his thoughts and opinions before they were finished making their point. As it happened, they spoke more slowly than he did and took longer to finish an idea than most of his other acquaintances. When he allowed them a little extra time, their discussions became more productive.

Step 4: He began to put his insights and observations about his five people into practice the very next day. Furthermore, he continued to work regularly on his listening plan and on other conversational issues.

Tom's Checklist

❏ People
❏ Problems
❏ Reasons
❏ Implementation

As Tom pursued the various objectives he had listed, he created a ripple effect. Ever-widening concentric circles of effective communicators were now revamping the culture of his company and his family. Almost imperceptibly at first, significant changes started to take place. In fact, the major changes occurred so gradually that no one could put a finger on their starting point. Even Tom wasn't entirely sure how the process had begun, and his specific role was quickly forgotten by others. Although he remained an unsung hero, Tom found he reaped great personal benefits, because his own circle of relationships had improved markedly. He reaped the rewards of becoming an expert in the Language of Effective Listening.

One person committed to listening effectively to just four or five others can start such a program. So join the human resources movement as Tom did! Set a timetable by which you expect to acquire a working knowledge of some of the skills. As Marge Blanchard says, "A goal without a timetable is just a dream." Though it may take years to become proficient in these skills, 30 days of consistent effort will produce positive results.

If you should run into a brick wall, rebound and try again. Not every try will be successful, but if you persist, you will have some good success. Success depends on your keeping at it. Don't bang your head against the wall, but do give full concentration and effort to whatever you are doing at the moment. Sticking to it means doing the tough things first and looking ahead for gratification and reward. It means being hungry for progress as a learner of the Language of Effective Listening. Do review your material, practice with the TV, then try again with your five key people. Success isn't guaranteed to the brilliant or the beautiful, only to the persistent.

The greatest quarterbacks complete only 6 out of 10 passes. Top oil companies using the consultation of expert geologists find oil in only 1 well in 10. A successful TV actor is turned down 29 out of 30 times when auditioning for roles in commercials. Winners in the stock market make money on only two out of five investments.

As you learn from your experience, you may need to reset your goals, timetable, or action plan. Ask yourself the following questions: (1) Will the skills I want to develop have a positive impact on my overall short-term and/or long-term purposes? (2) How will these skills help my company and my family? (3) Will these skills build better communication, quality relationships, and greater personal and professional productivity? Could I accept constructive criticism if I don't consistently follow through with my good intentions? (4) Should I communicate my action plan to those associates and specific family members with whom I intend to build better communication? If so, how?

If you decide to tell your associates what you are doing, don't be apologetic. Don't share too much. Do ask for their support. Ask them to let you know not only if you fail to do what you have committed yourself to do but also to let you know when you do use the Language of Effective Listening.

Through the 1990s and into the 21st century, managers will be hired and recognized more for their interpersonal skills than for their technical expertise. Those companies that incorporate progressive human resource programs and strategies will conduct the most successful operations.

Notes

Chapter 3: GIVE YOURSELF A SURPRISE

1. We adapted our criteria for self-examination from the pioneer work of Ralph Nichols, who was head of the Department of Rhetoric at the University of Minnesota, and Lyman Steil, Dr. Nichol's successor. Dr. Steil is the first president and founding father of The International Listening Association and President of Communication Development, Inc. Dr. Steil made the Ten Bad Habits available to Dr. Robertson in July 1980. See also, *Effective Listening, Key to Your Success*, Steil, Barker, and Watson, pp. 21–29.
2. Lyman Steil, July 1984.
3. Ted Plumb, August 1991.

Chapter 4: SUCCESS WITH CHALLENGE NUMBER ONE

1. Tom Peters, "Get Physical: Manage Space in Business Life," *Ossining Citizen Register*, December 1989.
2. Rene Dubos, quoted by Schuller, *Self-Esteem: The New Reformation*, pp. 18–19.
3. Bertram Brown, director of the National Institute of Mental Health, quoted by Schuller, *Self-Esteem: The New Reformation*, p. 106.

4. George Gallup Jr., quoted by Schuller, *Self-Esteem: The New Reformation*, p. 17.

5. Samuel Schreiner, Jr., in *The Reader's Digest*, February 1990, pp. 140–42.

6. Blood Pressure Study 1979, Society of Actuaries and Association of Life Insurance Medical Directors of America., quoted by Dr. Lynch, *The Language of the Heart*, New York: Basic Books, 1985, p. 56.

7. Lauchland A. Henry, *The Professional's Guide to Working Smarter*, quoted in *Sound View Executive Book Summaries*, July 1989, p. 4.

8. Harold Smith, "The 20% Activities that Bring 80% Payoff," *Training*, June 1978, p. 6.

9. Zig Ziglar, *Top Performance*, Old Tappan, N.J.: Fleming H. Revell, 1986, p. 129.

10. Otto Friedrich, "What Do Babies Know?" *Time*, 15 August 1983, pp. 54–55.

11. Denis Waitley, *Seeds of Greatness*, New York: Simon & Schuster, 1983, p. 110.

12. Kenneth Boa, personal conversation, 1987.

13. L. R. Wheeless quoted by Steil, Barker, and Watson, *Effective Listening, Key to Your Success*, p. 61.

14. L. K. Steil, *A Longitudinal Analysis of Listening Pedagogy in Minnesota Secondary Public Schools*, Ph.D. Dissertation, Wayne State University, Detroit, 1978, p. 43.

15. Denis Waitley, *Seeds of Greatness*, p. 87.

16. A concept created and used by Dr. Lyman Steil in his public workshops "Effective Listening: Key to Your Success."

Chapter 5: YOUR STAKE IN THE SPEAKER'S BOTTOM LINE

1. Lyman Steil shared these concepts with Dr. Robertson in July 1980 and subsequently.

2. Ibid.

3. Ibid.

4. Paul de Barros, writing assignments for Effective Communication and Development, 1980 ff.

Chapter 6: TROUBLESHOOTING

1. Dr. Robertson added two components to the original model created by Lyman Steil, creating a new model that includes the concepts of preparation and synchronization. For the original model see *Effective Listening, Key to Success,* Reading, Mass.: Addison-Wesley, 1983, by Steil, Barker, and Watson, pp. 21–29.

2. Ibid.

3. Bernard G. Guerney, Jr., "Relationship Enhancement, Marital/Family Therapy Training Program," April 6–9, 1990.

4. Paul de Barros, *Effective Communication and Development, Effective Listening Workshop Workbook,* p. 35.

5. Paul de Barros, ibid., p. 36.

6. David Augsburger, *Caring Enough to Hear and Be Heard,* Scottsdale: Herald Press, 1982, p. 52.

7. Suzette Haden Elgin, *The Last Word on the Gentle Art of Verbal Self-Defense,* Englewood Cliffs, N.J., 1983, p. 24.

8. David Augsburger, *Caring Enough to Hear and Be Heard,* p. 52.

9. "Laughter is the Best Medicine," *Reader's Digest,* n.d.

Chapter 7: *RELATIONS* AND ROADBLOCKS

1. Donald Osgood, *Breakthrough,* Old Tappan, N.J.: Fleming H. Revell, 1986, p. 14.

2. Richard Walters, personal interview, November 1982.

3. Bernard G. Guerney Jr., *Relationship Enhancement: Marital/Family Therapist's Manual*, pp. 100–1.

Chapter 8: THE CONTROL OF EMOTIONS

1. Lee Iacocca, *Iacocca, An Autobiography*, New York: Bantam Books, 1984, pp. 56–57.
2. Michael Maccoby, *Why Work*, New York: Simon & Schuster, 1988, p. 52.
3. Lyman K. Steil, personal interview, July 1980 and subsequently.
4. Suzette Haden Elgin, *The Gentle Art of Verbal Self-Defense*, Englewood Cliffs, N.J.: Prentice Hall, 1980, p. 11.
5. Paul de Barros, *Effective Communication and Development, Effective Listening Workshop Workbook*, 1981.
6. Suzette Haden Elgin, *The Last Word on the Gentle Art of Verbal Self-Defense*, p. 140.

Chapter 9: COMMUNISUASION: HOW TO LISTEN PERSUASIVELY

1. Donald V. Siebert, *The Ethical Executive: A Top C.E.O.'s Program for Success with the Corporate World*, p. 37.
2. Richard M. While Jr., *The Entrepreneur's Manual*, quoted by Alessandra and Wexler in *Non-Manipulative Selling*, p. 5.
3. David Augsburger, *Caring Enough to Hear and Be Heard*, Scottsdale: Herald Press, 1982, p. 65.
4. Siemens-Allis Sales Gram, n.d.
5. Suzette Haden Elgin, *The Gentle Art of Verbal Self-Defense*, Englewood Cliffs, N.J.: Prentice Hall, 1980, p. 193.

6. Sigmund Freud quoted by Alessandra & Wexler in *Non-Manipulative Selling*, Reston: Reston Publishing Company, 1979, p. 96.

7. Joseph Yeager Easten, N.L.P. Institute lecture, November 1985, New York.

8. Donald J. Moine and John H. Herd, *Modern Persuasion Strategies*, Englewood Cliffs, N.J.: Prentice Hall, 1984, p. 66.

9. Ibid., 60.

10. Jerry Richardson and Joel Margulis, *The Magic of Rapport*, San Francisco: Harbor Publishing, 1986, p. 19.

11. Michael McCaskey, "The Hidden Messengers Managers Send," *Harvard Business Review*, Nov./Dec. 1979, p. 147.

12. Robert and Dorothy Bolton quoted by Norman Wright in *Energize Your Life Through Total Communication*, pp. 69–70.

13. Suzette Haden Elgin, *The Last Word on Verbal Self-Defense*, p. 209.

14. William S. Condon quoted by Richardson and Margulis in *The Magic of Rapport*, p. 33.

15. Edward T. Hall quoted by Richardson & Margulis, *The Magic of Rapport*, p. 33.

16. Donald J. Moine and John H. Herd, *Modern Persuasion Techniques*, p. 29.

17. Suzette Haden Elgin, *The Gentle Art of Verbal Self-Defense*, p. 194.

18. Anthony Alessandra and Phillip S. Wexler, *Non-Manipulative Selling*, p. 6.

Chapter 10: SHARPEN YOUR NONVERBAL SKILLS

1. W. S. Condon, "The Relation of Interactional Synchrony to Cognitive and Emotional Processes," as quoted by Suzette Haden Elgin, *More on the Gentle Art of Verbal Self-Defense*, Englewood Cliffs, N.J.: Prenctice Hall, 1983, p. 219.

2. Suzette Haden Elgin, ibid., p. 220.

3. Ibid., p. 216.

4. Ibid., p. 203.

5. Lyman Steil, personal conversation, July 1980.

6. Fred Liedtke, "Humor in Uniform," *The Reader's Digest*, p. 77, n.d.

7. Daniel Coleman, *New York Times*, April 8, 1986. Report of a research project on nonverbal communication carried out by Peter Blanck and his associates and quoted by Suzette Haden Elgin, *Mastering the Gentle Art of Verbal Self-Defense*, p. 52.

8. Paul Ekman and Wallace V. Friesen, *Unmasking the Face*, Palo Alto: Consulting Psychologists Press, 1980, p. 5.

9. Ibid., p. 5.

10. Ibid., p. 88.

11. Ibid., p. 14.

12. Suzette Haden Elgin, *The Last Word on the Gentle Art of Verbal Self-Defense*, p. 217.

Chapter 11: IMPROVE LISTENING THROUGH EFFECTIVE NOTE TAKING

1. Ralph Nichols, *Are You Listening?* New York: McGraw-Hill, 1957, p. 114.

2. Nichols, ibid., pp. 113–114.

3. Nichols, ibid., pp. 115–116. In these pages Nichols has an excellent discussion on notetaking.

4. Dr. Lyman Steil, Dr. Larry Barker, and Dr. Kitty Watson, *Effective Listening, Key to Your Success*, Reading, Mass.: Addison-Wesley, 1983, pp. 110–114.

5. Steil, Barker, and Watson, ibid., p. 108.

6. Steil, Barker, and Watson, ibid., p. 20.

7. Paul de Barros, Effective Communication and Development, Inc., *Effective Listening Workshop Workbook,* 1980, p. 40.

8. de Barros, ibid., p. 40.

Bibliography

Alessandra, Anthony J., and Phillip S. Wexler with Jerry D. Deen, *Non-Manipulative Selling*. Reston: Reston Publishing Company, 1979.

Augsburger, David. *Caring Enough To Hear and Be Heard*, Scottdale: Herald Press, 1982.

Bandler, Richard and John Grinder. *Frogs into Princes*. Moab: Real People Press, 1979.

Blood Pressure Study, 1979, Society of Actuaries and Assn. of Life Insurance Medical Directors of America: November, 1980.

Boa, Kenneth. Personal Conversations, 1981–90.

Burley-Allen, Madelyn. *Listening: The Forgotten Skill*. New York: John Wiley & Sons, 1982.

Campolo, Anthony Jr., *The Success Fantasy*. Wheaton: Victor Books, 1980.

Coakley, Carolyn G., and Andrew D. Wolvin. *Listening*. Dubuque, IA: Wm. C. Brown Publishers, 1992.

de Barros, Paul. Writing assignments for Effective Communication and Development, 1980 ff.

Delmar, Ken. *Winning Moves*. New York: Warner Books, 1984.

Demaray, Donald E. *Laughter, Joy, and Healing*. Grand Rapids: Baker Book House Co., 1986.

Dobson, James. *Emotions: Can You Trust Them?* Ventura: Gospel Light, 1980.

Ekman, Paul, and Wallace V. Friesen. *Unmasking the Face: A Guide to Recognizing Emotions from Facial Expressions*. Palo Alto: Consulting Psychologists Press, 1984.

Elgin, Suzette Haden. *The Gentle Art of Verbal Self-Defense*. Englewood Cliffs, N.J.: Prentice Hall, 1980.

Elgin, Suzette Haden. *The Gentle Art of Verbal Self-Defense Workbook.* New York: Dorset, 1987.

Elgin, Suzette Haden. *More on the Gentle Art of Verbal Self-Defense.* Englewood Cliffs, N.J.: Prentice Hall, 1983.

Frankl, Viktor E. *Man's Search for Meaning.* New York: Pocket Books, Simon & Schuster, 1963.

Friedrich, Otto. "What Do Babies Know?" *Time.* 15 August 1983.

Geeting, Bakter, and Corinne. *How to Listen Assertively.* New York: Simon & Schuster, 1976.

Glasser, William Jr., M.D. *Reality Therapy.* New York: Harper & Row, 1965.

Guerney, Bernard G., Jr. *Relationship Enhancement.* San Francisco: Jossey-Bass, 1977.

Guerney, Bernard G., Jr. *Relationship Enhancement: Marital/Family Therapist's Manual,* 2nd ed. State College: 1976.

Guerney, Bernard G., Jr. *Relationship Enhancement: Marital/Family Therapy Training Program.* State College

Henry, Lauchland A. *The Professional Guide to Working Smarter.* Tenafly, N.J.: Berrill-Ellsworth Associates, Inc.

Holy Bible, New International Version. New York: Oxford University Press, 1984.

Iacocca, Lee, with William Novak. *Iacocca: An Autobiography.* New York: Bantam Books, 1984.

Keffe, W. F. *Listen Management.* New York: McGraw-Hill, 1971.

"Laughter is the Best Medicine." *The Reader's Digest.* Pleasantville: May 1990.

Liedtke, Fred. "Humor in Uniform" *Reader's Digest.* Pleasantville: n.d.

Lynch, James J. *The Language of the Heart.* New York: Basic Books, 1985.

Maccoby, Michael. *Why Work.* New York: Simon & Schuster, 1988.

Malandro, Loretta A., and Larry Barker. *Non-Verbal Communication.* Reading, Mass.: Addison-Wesley Publishing, 1983.

McCasky, Michael. "The Hidden Messengers Managers Send," *Harvard Business Review,* Nov./Dec. 1979.

Mehrabian, Albert. *Nonverbal Communication*. Chicago: Aldine-Atherton, 1972.

Moine, Donald J., and John H. Herd. *Modern Persuasion Strategies*. Englewood Cliffs, N.J.: Prentice Hall, 1984.

Nichols, Ralph G., and Leonard A. Stevens. *Are You Listening?* New York: McGraw-Hill, 1957.

Nierenberg, Gerard I. *The Art of Negotiating*. New York: Simon & Schuster, 1968.

Nierenberg, Gerard and Henry H. Calero. *How to Read a Person Like a Book*. New York: Simon & Schuster, 1971.

Osgood, Donald W. *Breaking Through*. Old Tappan, N.J.: Fleming H. Revell, 1986.

Peale, Norman Vincent. *Positive Imaging*. Old Tappan, N.J.: Fleming H. Revell, 1982.

Peter, Lawrence J. *The Laughter Prescription*. New York: Ballantine Books, Random House, 1982.

Peters, Tom. "Get Physical: Manage Space in Business Life," *Ossining Citizen Register*, December 1989.

Petersen, Roger. Writing Assignments for Effective Communication and Development, Inc., 1989ff.

Richardson, Jerry, and Joel Margulis. *The Magic of Rapport*. San Francisco: Harbor Publishing, 1986.

Robertson, Arthur K. *Effective Listening Workbook*. New York: Effective Communication & Development, Inc., 1988.

Schreiner, Samuel, Jr. "A Question That Can Save Marriages." *Reader's Digest*, Pleasantville: February, 1990.

Schreiner, Samuel, Jr. *The Reader's Digest*, Pleasantville: February, 1990.

Schuller, Robert H. *Self-Esteem: The New Reformation*. Waco: Word Books, 1982.

Seimens-Allis. *Sales Gram*. Vol. 1, Number 3, n.d.

Siebert, Donald V. *The Ethical Executive: A Top C.E.O.'s Program for Success with the Corporate World*.

Simon, Sidney B. *Negative Criticism*. Niles: Argus Communications, 1978.

Smith, Dr. Harold. "The 20% Activities That Bring 80% Payoff." *Training*, June 1978.

Soundview Executive Book Summaries. Bristol: 1989.

Steil, Lyman K. *A Longitudinal Analysis of Listening Pedagogy in Minnesota Secondary Public Schools.* Ph.D. Dissertation, Wayne State University, Detroit, 1978.

Steil, Lyman K. Personal conversations, 1980ff.

Steil, Lyman K., Larry L. Barker, and Kitty W. Watson. *Effective Listening.* Reading, Mass.: Addison-Wesley Publishing, 1983.

Steil, Lyman K., JoAnne Summerfield, and George deMare. *Listening—It Can Change Your Life.* New York: John Wiley & Sons, 1983.

Waitley, Denis. *The Psychology of Winning.* New York: Berkeley Books, 1984.

Waitley, Denis. *Seeds of Greatness.* New York: Simon & Schuster, 1983.

Waitley, Denis. *The Winner's Edge.* New York: Berkley Books, 1980.

Walters, Richard. Personal Consultation on Listening Workshop, 1981 ff.

Walters, Walter. Personal interview, November, 1981.

Wolff, Florence I., Nadine Marsnik, William S. Tacey, and Ralph G. Nichols. *Perceptive Listening.* New York: Holt, Rinehart & Winston, 1983.

Wright, H. Norman. *Energize Your Life Through Total Communication.* Old Tappan, N.J.: Fleming H. Revell, 1986.

Yeager, Joseph. Eastern Neurolinguistics Institute, Certification Training, April 1985–February 1986.

Ziglar, Zig. *Top Performance.* Old Tappan, N.J.: Fleming H. Revell, 1986.

Index

1. How did you find out about this Briefcase Book?

☐ Bookstore ☐ Irwin Catalog
☐ Advertisement ☐ Convention
☐ Flyer ☐ Other Catalog
☐ Sales Rep
other _____

2. Was this book provided by your organization or did you purchase this book for yourself?

☐ individual purchase
☐ organizational purchase

3. Are you using this book as a part of a training program?

☐ yes ☐ no

4. Did this book meet your expectations?

☐ yes ☐ no

(please explain)_____
_____
_____
_____

5. What other topics would you like to see addressed in this series?

(Please list)

_____
_____
_____

6. ☐ *Please have a sales representative call me.*

I am interested in:
☐ bulk purchase discounts
☐ custom publishing

7. ☐ *Please send me a catalog of your products.*

_____
Name

_____
Title

_____
Organization

_____
Address

_____
City, State, Zip

_____
Phone